ARTIFICIAL INTELLIGENCE

Rise
Survive
&
Thrive
In An AI-Powered World

First Edition

CORLISS WILLETT COLLINS
BSHIM, RHIT, CRCR, CSM, CAIP

Artificial Intelligence

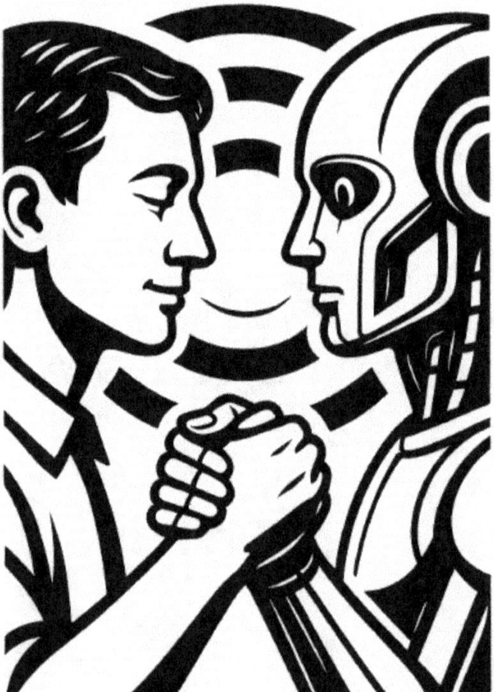

Rise, Survive & Thrive Together

In an AI-Powered World

"DO NOT FEAR A FUTURE WITH AI—
AUTOMATE, COLLABORATE, TAKE THE LEAD
AND SHAPE IT."

--- *Ms. Co Co*

TABLE OF CONTENTS

FOREWORD

Every so often, a book arrives that is not just timely but *urgent. Artificial Intelligence: Rise, Survive & Thrive in an AI-Powered World* is that book.

We are living in unprecedented times. Artificial Intelligence is no longer a futuristic concept whispered about in Silicon Valley boardrooms or science fiction novels. It is here—woven into our daily lives, influencing decisions we make, shaping economies, transforming work, and redefining what it means to be human in the 21st century. And yet, for all its impact, many remain unprepared for the AI revolution unfolding around them.

That is where this book comes in.

What Ms. Collins has accomplished with *Artificial Intelligence: Rise, Survive & Thrive in an AI-Powered World* is extraordinary. This is not just another book about technology; it is a guidebook for human relevance in an AI-driven age. It teaches us how to navigate this technological shift with wisdom, adaptability, and ethical courage. It reminds us that the future does not belong to the strongest or even the smartest—it belongs to those who are most adaptable.

The pages you are about to read do more than explain AI—they empower you to understand how to partner with it. Ms. Collins breaks down complex AI concepts into clear, actionable insights. Whether you are a business leader trying to future-proof your company, a healthcare professional navigating AI-powered systems, or an everyday citizen curious (or concerned) about what's next, this book meets you where you are and lifts you higher.

Most importantly, this is a book about **thriving**, not just surviving. It challenges the reader to rise with AI, not fear it; to collaborate. We are at the forefront of technological advancement.

As someone who has spent decades working with AI-powered technologies, studying innovation, leadership, and ethics, I can tell you: this is the kind of resource I wish every person would read before AI becomes so embedded in society that it is too late to influence how it is being used.

If you are ready to embrace the AI era with eyes wide open, to engage critically and creatively, and to secure your new place in this world, you are holding the right book.

Let the journey begin.

Guilinda Gonzalez, MS-RHIT

Chief Health Information Management

VA Medical Center

PREFACE

This book was born out of both a professional journey and a personal conviction.

I have worked with AI-powered technologies for more than fifteen years. As someone who has spent years working at the crossroads of healthcare quality, compliance, and artificial intelligence automation, I have witnessed a dual reality: AI holds the promise of revolutionizing the way we work, how we look at information, process data, care for people, and power our industries—but only if we build, implement, and govern it with foresight and responsibility.

When I first began exploring AI-powered solutions within the Revenue Cycle Management space, it was not about the hype. It was about wanting to understand AI, Master it, and Utilize it to solve real problems that impact lives, not just ledgers. It was about asking, *Can AI make this easier, safer, and better?*

But as innovation surged, so did my concerns. I saw systems being deployed without transparency, without proper quality, compliance, and regulatory policies, procedures, and oversight. I saw decision-making being handed over to algorithms, with only a few who understand AI. And I saw a troubling gap between those who shape AI and those who are most affected by it.

That is when this book started to take shape.

Artificial Intelligence is now everywhere—on our smartphones, in our homes, hospitals, schools, on our jobs, and even in our headlines. But beyond the hype, a deeper question lingers:

What is the real story behind who AI is, and what AI is doing?

So, let us begin with the truth as I understand it: **AI is not a person**. It has no soul, no conscience, no dreams or desires. It does not *want* anything. AI is a mirror, a tool built by humans, trained on human data, and shaped by human intentions. AI can be programmed to be very helpful or cause harm. What it "does" depends entirely on the hands that develop it, the goals that drive it, and the guardrails—or lack thereof—that govern it.

And yet, it acts. It writes code, answers questions, diagnoses diseases, documents and codes patient visits to the doctor, drives cars, invests your hard-earned money, learns how you do your job, and takes the controls. AI is now even making decisions about who gets hired, fired, insured, or incarcerated. It performs feats that were once only imagined in science fiction just a few years ago. It holds power, not because it is alive, but because **we have given it power**.

In that power lies the paradox.

Leaders who are advancing AI promise that it will elevate our world, solve problems faster than ever, reduce errors in medicine, outperform humans, improve processes and performance in personalized learning and professional development, and unlock the next wave of scientific discoveries. But, at what cost?

AI also poses an existential threat to disseminate disinformation and misinformation; it is being used to erode privacy, displace millions of workers, minimize the value of explicit populations, and exacerbate inequality, all while operating behind layers of complexities and experiential promises that most people do not pay attention to or fully understand.

So, what is my story? Why did I decide to write this book at this time?

Artificial Intelligence: Rise, Survive, and Thrive in an AI-Powered World is my response to the gaps and urgency associated with this phenomenon called AI. It is a call to action—and a roadmap—for everyday people, including blue-collar workers, white-collar professionals, legal scholars, ethical front-runners, students, small-to-mid-size business owners, healthcare leaders, developers, educators, and all who refuse to be left behind in this AI revolution.

This book is not meant to scare you. Instead, it should empower you, with strategies to *rise* as leaders, to survive *the chaos of rapid transformation, and ultimately to thrive—economically, ethically, and collectively,* in a world increasingly shaped by AI, Algorithms, and Intelligent Systems.

If you are holding this book, you most likely have an interest in learning more or have been searching for answers about AI, because you sense the world is changing at an accelerated pace, and you want to keep up with it. You can use this book to facilitate discussions with your family, friends, colleagues, and the community.

Let us all choose to rise, survive, and thrive together wisely, with courage, vision, and a shared mission to succeed in this AI-powered world. I hope you will be inspired to use AI for good.

—Corliss Willett Collins | BSHIM, RHIT, CRCR, CCA, CAIMC, CAIP, CSM

[Also known as Ms. Co. Co]

ACKNOWLEDGEMENTS

"I want to thank God, My Partner in Life, Our Daughters, Our Sons, My Mom, Stepmom, Dad, Our Grandchildren, Our Great-Grandchildren, and all other family members who breathed life into the essence of who I am today. Our Ancestors. Our Lineage of Faith and Traditions that was passed on to us, and still being cultivated by us, and all Future Generations, and the Publisher. Thank you!

To every single employer who hired me and allowed me to be a servant leader on their Revenue Cycle Management (RCM) teams, encouraged me, sent positive thoughts my way, or just inspired me to be a better version of myself. Thank you!

A MESSAGE TO OUR READERS

"We are living in a defining moment of history. As AI reshapes our world, remember this: the future is not just something we enter—it is something that we help to create by taking action, or by sitting on the sidelines and doing nothing. Either way, we are all contributors!

Moreover, if we choose to lead with purpose, adapt with courage, and shape a future that reflects the very best of who we are, we will all be blessed for it!"

DISCLAIMER

The information presented in this book is intended for educational and informational purposes only. While every effort has been made to ensure the accuracy and reliability of the content, the author and publisher make no representations or warranties regarding the completeness, suitability, or applicability of any ideas, methodologies, or strategies discussed.

This book does not constitute professional, legal, financial, medical, or technological advice. Readers are encouraged to seek the guidance of qualified professionals, tailored to their specific circumstances. The author and publisher disclaim any liability, loss, or risk incurred as a consequence, directly or indirectly, for the use and application of any of the contents of this book.

Furthermore, any examples, case studies, scenarios, or predictions are for illustrative purposes only and should not be construed as a guarantee of future outcomes. References to companies, organizations, platforms, or technologies are made for educational purposes and do not imply endorsement or affiliation unless specifically stated.

All trademarks, service marks, copyrights, and trade names are the property of their respective owners.

By reading this book, you acknowledge and accept that the content provided is "as is" without any guarantees or warranties of any kind, expressed or implied.

CHAPTER ONE:
Introduction

The History of Artificial Intelligence

With all the conversations surrounding AI today, it's easy to believe that artificial intelligence is a modern product of the digital revolution. But the truth is that, conceptually, AI has been around for ages. Sure, the advent may have some novelty in its applications in the real world, but the idea and the scientific roots date back thousands of years. AI's history is a tapestry woven from philosophy, mathematics, cognitive science, and computing.

This chapter charts the chronological evolution of AI, spotlighting key milestones, figures, breakthroughs, and shifts in ideology. Understanding AI's past helps us grasp the trajectory of where we are headed in the future.

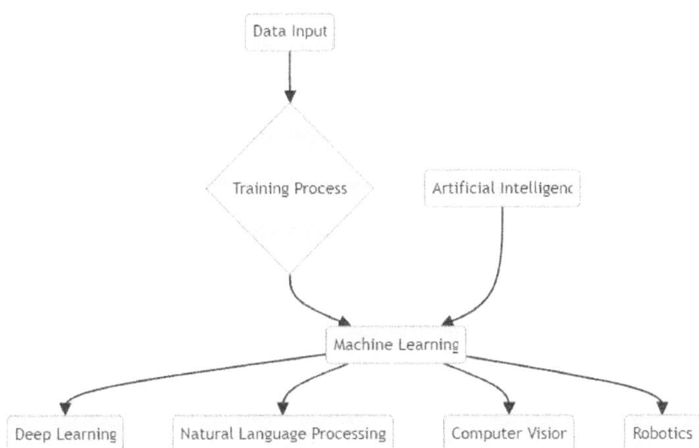

Fig. 1: "Understanding AI and Algorithms Workflow"

1. Early Concepts of Machine Intelligence (Antiquity – 1800s)

Myth and Mechanism

- **Ancient Greece**: Myths like *Talos*, a bronze giant built to protect Crete, reveal early imaginings of artificial life.
- **China**: The *Yan Shi automaton* described in Liezi (c. 3rd century BCE) portrays a human-like mechanical figure.
- **Islamic Golden Age**: Engineers like *Al-Jazari* (12th century) constructed programmable automata for entertainment and function.

These early stories and inventions represent humanity's perennial fascination with creating intelligent beings.

---

2. Theoretical Foundations (1600s – 1900s)

Rationalism and Logic

- **René Descartes (1637)** imagined animals and possibly humans as complex machines in *Discourse on the Method*.
- **Gottfried Wilhelm Leibniz** introduced the idea of a universal language of reasoning, influencing later symbolic logic.

Mathematics Meets Mechanism

- **George Boole** (1854) developed Boolean algebra, providing a framework for digital logic.
- **Alan Turing** (1936) proposed the *Turing Machine*, theorizing a machine that could compute anything computable, laying the groundwork for AI.

🧠 *Turing's work bridged the gap between abstract computation and machine-based reasoning.*

---

3. The Birth of AI as a Field (1950s – 1960s)

Defining the Vision

- **Alan Turing's "Computing Machinery and Intelligence" (1950)** asked: *Can machines think?* This essay birthed the *Turing Test* for machine intelligence.
- **1956 Dartmouth Conference**: Organized by *John McCarthy*, *Marvin Minsky*, *Claude Shannon*, and *Nathaniel Rochester*, this event coined the term "artificial intelligence" and launched AI as an academic discipline.

Early Achievements

- **Logic Theorist** (1955) by Newell and Simon proved mathematical theorems.
- **ELIZA** (1966) by Joseph Weizenbaum simulated conversation—a precursor to modern chatbots.

📚 *"As soon as it works, no one calls it AI anymore." – John McCarthy*

---

4. The Rise and Fall of Expectations (1970s – 1980s)

An AI Winter

Despite early enthusiasm, progress slowed due to:

- Limited computing power.
- Overpromised capabilities.
- Failure of expert systems to scale effectively.

Funding dropped, leading to what is now known as the **First AI Winter** (1974–1980), followed by a **Second AI Winter** in the late 1980s.

Expert Systems Boom

In between winters, AI found success in *expert systems* like XCON, which encoded domain knowledge via rules.

🧩 These systems worked in narrow domains but lacked flexibility and learning capability.

---

5. The Machine Learning Revolution (1990s – 2010s)

Statistical Learning Takes Over

- Shift from symbolic AI to **machine learning** (ML), driven by:
    - Larger datasets.
    - Advances in algorithms (e.g., decision trees, SVMs).
    - Increased computing power.

Key Milestones

- **IBM's Deep Blue** defeated world chess champion *Garry Kasparov* (1997).
- **DARPA Grand Challenges** pushed forward autonomous driving (2004–2007).
- **ImageNet (2012)** and the rise of **deep learning** via *AlexNet* dramatically improved computer vision.

🔍 *Deep learning mimics the brain's structure through artificial neural networks.*

---

6. Modern AI: The Age of Foundation Models (2015–Present)

AI Goes Mainstream

- **Natural Language Processing (NLP)**:
  - Tools like *GPT*, *BERT*, and *Claude* can generate and understand human-like text.
- **Computer Vision**:
  - Facial recognition, image classification, and video analysis now outperform humans in some tasks.
- **AI in Practice**:
  - From medicine and finance to transportation and entertainment, AI is integrated into everyday life.

Notable Breakthroughs

- **AlphaGo**
  - By DeepMind defeated Go champion *Lee Sedol* (2016).
- **OpenAI's GPT-3 (2020)**, **GPT-4 (2023),** and **GPT-5 (2025)**
  - Demonstrated unprecedented generative capabilities.
- **Multimodal AI models**
  - Began interpreting images, audio, and text together.

🌐 *AI is no longer a niche—it has become an infrastructure woven into the tapestry of our lives… The question is it compliant, ethical, and safe?*

---

7. Ethical Reckonings and the Future (2020s and Beyond)

Ethics, Bias, and Alignment

- As AI capabilities surge, concerns grow around:
    - Algorithmic bias.
    - Privacy violations.
    - Job displacement.
    - Autonomous weapons.
    - AI sentience and alignment.

Global initiatives, such as the EU AI Act, the U.S. AI Executive Order, and the OECD AI, are like slow-moving trains. Although principles are emerging to guide the responsible development of AI ethics, quality, compliance, and legal standards underpin the advancements being made.

Along with the progress of machines, the history of AI also maps human imagination and the will to bring it to fruition. It is fascinating to see how AI has come from mechanical dreams of the ancient world to the ubiquitous systems we have today.

As we enter an era where AI is reshaping our entire way of life—without exaggeration—the knowledge of where we have been will serve as a compass for where we must go.

⚖ *The future of AI hinges not just on what it can do, but what it should do.*

CHAPTER TWO:
Rise with AI

Finding New Opportunities in an Automated World

Artificial Intelligence is not coming; it is already here. As the last chapter details, AI has come from being a far-fetched, pie-in-the-sky fantasy to being a very real thing. But while many fear employment displacement, the true leaders are learning to rise **with AI**, not against it.

This chapter is about seizing that moment.

"AI will not replace you. But a person using AI to their advantage will."

This phrase has become a modern mantra, and for good reason. The rise of AI is not replacing human capability; it is expanding it. Those who learn how to collaborate with AI will find themselves at the forefront of innovation, productivity, and success.

The Shift: From AI Disruption to AI Partnership

Historically, technological revolutions have caused seismic shifts in the labor force, from the Industrial Revolution to the rise of the internet. AI is doing something similar, but with a key distinction:

AI is a collaborative supplement, not a replacement.

Examples of AI Partnership:

- **Healthcare:**
  Doctors are utilizing AI-powered diagnostic tools to identify early signs of disease more quickly and with greater precision.
- **Finance:**
  Analysts are leveraging AI algorithms to scan markets and predict trends in real time.
- **Entrepreneurship:**
  Small business owners are using AI to automate marketing, customer service, and data insights—saving time and multiplying impact.

The rise of AI does not have to mean obsolescence; it can mean **opportunity**—if you are willing to adapt.

Mindset Shift: From Fear to Forward Thinking

Here is the uncomfortable truth: fear of AI is often rooted in a lack of knowledge and understanding.

When you experience AI as a black box issue (lack of transparency or explainability), it is easy to fall into fear narratives—worrying about job loss, automation threats, or loss of control. But once you develop **insight into how AI works**, you regain power. You shift from fear to strategic foresight.

Key Mindset Shifts from Fear to a Rise with AI:

Old Thinking	New Thinking
"AI will take my job."	"AI will help me complete tasks. It will not take my job."
"I don't understand AI."	"I will learn enough to lead with AI, not fear it."
"AI is too complicated."	"AI is a tool, like email once was. Learn the basics, leverage the rest."

⚖ Strategy + Approach + Results → Achieving Desired Outcomes Successfully!

Rise with AI: Practical Strategies

Here are actionable steps you can take today to prepare yourself and your organization for an AI-powered future.

1. Develop AI Literacy Action Plan

You do not need to become a data scientist to work with AI, but you do need to understand the basics.

- **Learn the Language of AI**
  Understand terms like machine learning, natural language processing, predictive analytics, and generative AI.

Resource Suggestion: You can find free online courses on Coursera, edX, or Google's AI Basics for Everyone.

Understand AI's Capabilities and Limits
Know what AI can do today—and where human judgment will be essential tomorrow.

2. Identify Tasks AI Can Enhance

Look at your daily work. Which tasks are repetitive, time-consuming, or pattern-based? These are prime candidates for AI support.

Examples of AI Enhancements

- Drafting emails or reports
- Automating data entry
- Summarizing large documents
- Analyzing customer trends
- Automating appointment scheduling

---

3. Integrate AI into Your Workflow

Start small. Use AI tools in your daily tasks:

- **Productivity:** Chatbots, transcription tools, meeting summarizers
- **Marketing:** AI-driven content generation, ad optimization
- **Operations:** AI-assisted data analytics, customer service automation

The goal is never to replace your role, but to free up time for high-value, creative, and strategic work.

---

4. Stay Ethical and Human-Centered

AI can enhance your work, but it must align with ethical standards. Be mindful of:

- Data privacy
- Bias mitigation
- Transparency
- Human-in-the-loop oversight

By rising with AI responsibly, you ensure that technology serves the people you love, respect, and care about (our global society) —not the other way around.

Case Study: The Entrepreneur Who Rose with AI

Meet Carla, a small business owner running a boutique marketing agency. Two years ago, she was overwhelmed, managing content calendars, data analytics, and client pitches alone.

Today, Carla uses AI to:

- Automate social media content generation
- Use AI analytics to spot client trends
- Generate personalized marketing reports in minutes

Result? Her business has tripled in size, but her workload hasn't. Carla did not fear AI—she learned to work **with it**.

The Choice Is Yours

AI will continue to evolve at an exponential speed. You can choose to resist it and risk falling behind—or you can embrace the change, build new skills, and **Rise with AI**.

Remember: **It is not about competing with machines. It is about learning to lead alongside them.**

Reader Reflection

Here's what you should take away from this chapter:

1. AI is a partner, not a replacement.
2. Upskilling in AI literacy is essential, not optional.
3. Ethical, human-centered AI use will define future leadership opportunities.

Reader Strategy | People Powered Intelligence (PPI)

Here are a few things you can do to warm up to AI adoption in your life:

1. Choose one AI tool to integrate into your daily routine this week.
2. Sign up for an AI fundamentals course (Use the Diagram below for ideas)
3. Reflect: Which tool do you think would help you work smarter, not harder with AI?

Fig. 2: Rise with AI Diagram

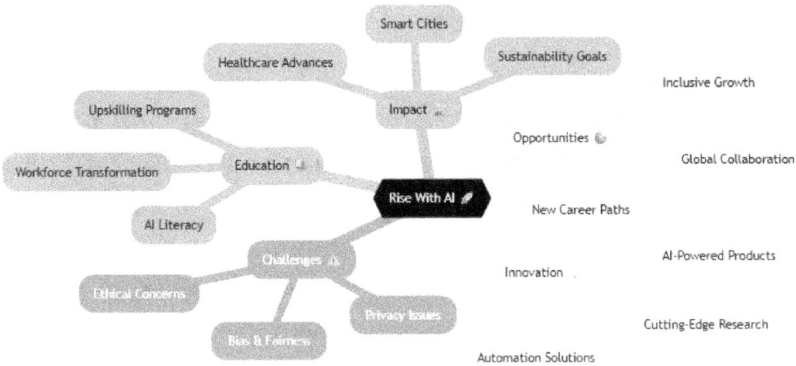

CHAPTER THREE:
What is AI Literacy, and Why Does it Matter?

The Invisible Revolution

AI's revolution is only as invisible as air: you cannot see it, but you can see everything that sways and waves in its effect. Artificial Intelligence is quietly transforming the world around us. It is writing emails, coding doctor's visits, predicting traffic patterns, and even helping judges determine bail decisions. Yet, despite its reach, some people are either unaware that they are interacting with AI or lack the understanding to engage with it critically.

AI has transcended its niche-specific, purpose-built space and has become a societal force, intertwined with how we work, learn, shop, vote, and even care for our families. In other words, AI is everywhere. This makes **AI literacy** one of the most important life skills that we need to develop in the 21st century.

I am getting flashbacks of the conversations we used to have about the internet back in the 90's. Or smartphones and social media in the early 2010s. This is our opportunity to lead!

I. Defining AI Literacy

The sheer everywhere-ness of AI doesn't mean that all of us have to suddenly become data scientists. But it's essential to understand AI technologies, learn how they work, their capabilities, and how to collaborate with them effectively.

Just like literacy in reading and writing empowered citizens during the Industrial Age, **AI literacy will define civic, economic, and personal power in the AI Age**.

Fig. 3: AI Literacy and Collaboration Workflow

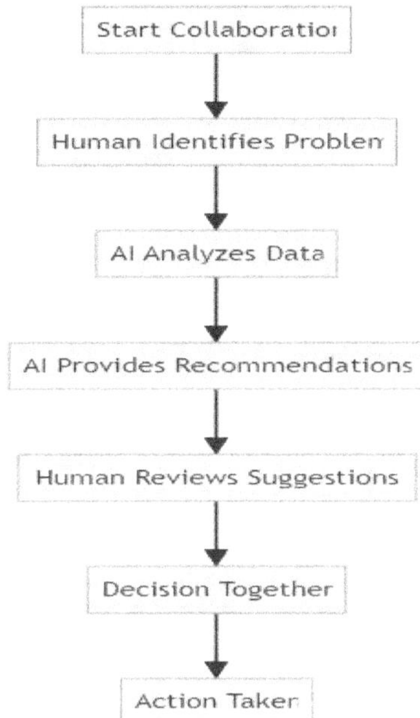

II. The Pillars of AI Literacy

Of course, AI literacy is not a one-step process. There's a lot of depth to explore, which can be overwhelming. So, I've broken it down into pillars. Let's explore each pillar in greater depth:

1. Foundational Knowledge

1.1 Understanding the Basic Mechanics of AI:

i. It starts with the Algorithm. An **algorithm** is a **step-by-step set of instructions or rules** designed to solve a problem or perform a specific task.

ii. **AI training data** refers to the **information (text, images, audio, video, or structured**

data) used to **teach an artificial intelligence (AI) system how to perform a specific task** and perform **predictive analysis**.

iii. **Deep Learning** is a **subset of machine learning** that uses **artificial neural networks** with many layers (hence "deep") to learn patterns from large volumes of data.

1.2 Five Key Characteristics of an Algorithm

i. **Well-defined steps**
   - Each instruction is unambiguous

ii. **Input**
   - An Algorithm must have zero or more well-defined inputs

iii. **Output**
   - An Algorithm must produce at least one specific, measurable output or result.

iv. **Finiteness**
   - It must complete and terminate after a finite number of steps.

v. **Effectiveness**
   - All operations in the Algorithm must be feasible and practically executable.

1.3 Core Features

i. Mimics the human brain (with layers of neurons).

ii. Learns from raw data (images, sound, text) without needing manual feature selection.

iii. Requires **large datasets** and **high computing power**.

Examples:

- **Input:** Patient demographics in RCM, procedure codes, or claims data
- **Output**: A CPT code recommendation, a claim denial prediction, or a revenue forecast

A lack of understanding could lead to preventable errors, poor quality, and failure to meet compliance standards, neither of which fosters healthy, productive, or profitable engagement opportunities for all parties involved.

2. What is Algorithmic Thinking exactly?

Algorithmic Thinking is the ability to **break down a problem into a clear, logical sequence of steps** that can be followed to solve the issue at hand, often with an end goal of designing a specified type of algorithm.

2.1 What data does the AI need to complete these steps?

It depends on **what the AI is being trained to do.**

2.2 What might AI miss during the process of performing Training Model steps?

Regulatory Context in Data: AI learns from the data it is fed. If the data has issues, AI misses important nuances. That means AI can predict what's "likely" but miss what's *legal*. **AI has its limitations, and several important aspects may be overlooked.**

2.3 What happens when the data is incorrect, incomplete, or biased?

As stated in section 2.2, when AI is trained or operates on **incorrect, incomplete, or biased data**, it can lead to **serious errors, inefficiencies, and even harm.**

3. What happens when AI Data is flawed?

3.1 Incorrect Data Leads to Defective Decisions and Poor Performance

- **Impact:** AI learns or predicts based on the training models that humans create. Wrong facts could cause significant harm.

  Examples:

  - A healthy patient's chart could be mislabeled as having cancer
  - A legitimate insurance claim payment could be denied based on an incorrect diagnosis code.

3.2 Incomplete Data Leads to Limited Understanding

- **Impact:** The AI only sees part of the picture, leading to inaccurate or generalized outputs.

  Examples:

  - AI overlooks at-risk patients due to predictive analysis, hospital readmission, and socio-economic data misses.
  - An AI chatbot missing key regulatory updates gives generic answers in error.

3.3 Biased Data Leads to Unfair Outcomes

- **Impact:** AI unfortunately discriminates against certain groups and outcomes.

  Examples:

  - Hiring algorithms favor resumes from men vs. women due to biased historical data.
  - Medical AI underdiagnoses skin conditions in darker skin tones because it was primarily trained on light skin images.

3.4 Real-World Consequences:

Domain	Potential Harm
Healthcare	Misdiagnosis, unequal treatment, and denial of care
Finance	Biased loan approvals, inaccurate credit scoring
Legal	Racial bias in sentencing algorithms
Business	Poor forecasting, flawed automation, and customer dissatisfaction

Summary:

Any AI model is only as good as the data it is trained on. When AI is fed **insufficient data**, it yields poor **results**, often at scale. To build **trustworthy AI**, the data must be **accurate, complete, and fair**. We have seen the backlash Google's AI bot, Gemini, received back in 2023, which was the perfect example of training on bad data. Both Ethical Reasoning and Human-AI Collaboration are strongly recommended.

Ethical Reasoning is Critical

- Every AI decision has an ethical implication. Literacy means understanding that:
  - AI can amplify existing inequalities
  - Systems trained on biased data will often reproduce that bias
  - Transparency and explainability are non-negotiable in critical systems (healthcare revenue cycle management, finance, policing)

Human-AI Collaboration is Recommended

- AI is not a replacement—it is a collaborator. Literacy means learning to:
  - Prompt AI tools effectively
  - Verify and cross-check outputs
  - Know when to delegate to AI and when to override it

III. Case Studies: The Risks of AI Illiteracy

As you can now understand, relying on AI tools without the necessary AI literacy education and training could have detrimental effects. Let's explore the possibility of what could happen when AI literacy is lacking:

- **Case 1: The Resumé Filter**
    - A major tech company used an AI tool to screen job applications. Unbeknownst to them, it had learned to downgrade résumés from women, because it had been trained on 10 years of male-dominated hiring data.
- **Case 2: Predictive Policing**
    - In cities like Los Angeles and Chicago, AI models were used to predict where crimes are likely to occur. However, these systems disproportionately targeted neighborhoods with high historic police activity, creating a cycle of over-policing.
- **Case 3: Medical Misdiagnosis**
    - A health app powered by generative AI advised a patient with chest pain that they were likely experiencing indigestion. The AI was trained on "limited symptom data" and failed to suggest a possible heart attack. Proper patient care was delayed.

Each case reveals what is at stake: **bias, injustice, risk, and even loss of life** when AI literacy is not present at the user, developer, or policy level.

IV. AI Literacy as a Civic Right

AI literacy is no longer a luxury—it is a **civic literacy right** akin to employment, financial, or media literacy. Those who understand AI will:

- Better navigate the labor market
- Make smarter consumer and healthcare decisions

- Spot manipulation in digital media
- Advocate for better public policy

Those without it will be:

- Misinformed
- Manipulated by algorithms
- Disadvantaged in job opportunities
- Silenced by automated systems.
    - What you do not know could cause harm to you and your loved ones!

In a digital democracy, **algorithmic transparency and informed citizenship must go hand in hand.** When it does not, everyone suffers the consequences. We are all in this together!

V. Building a More AI-Literate Society

What can you and Institutions do?

A Great Place to Start

- Introduce AI concepts in K-12 STEM and humanities classes
- Teach students how social media platforms use algorithms to shape perception
- Offer Ethics Training alongside computer science

Businesses

- Train employees on AI tools and their limitations
- Conduct regular algorithm audits for accuracy, quality, fairness, and bias
- Involve non-technical staff in AI tool adoption

Governments

- Fund public AI education initiatives
- Make government AI models open-source and explainable
- Protect citizens from algorithmic harm through regulation

Individuals

- Stay curious—explore free courses and media on AI
- Understand the risks of facial recognition, credit scoring, and surveillance tools
- Use AI tools thoughtfully, and never stop asking: *Who built this? Who benefits? Who is harmed?*

- Encourage the schools in your community, workplace, or state government to invest in responsible AI education and its responsible use.

Reader Reflection

Now that you have a better understanding of how AI works and the impact it has, ask yourself:

1. What role is AI playing in my life that I may be unaware of?

2. Do I rely on AI tools without understanding how they work?
3. Have I ever challenged or questioned an AI decision before accepting it?

Reader Strategy | People Powered Intelligence (PPI)

Here's a bit of homework for you from this chapter.

1. **Audit Your AI Exposure**:
    - List the AI tools you use daily—ChatGPT, Google Maps, Netflix, social media feeds. Learn how they work.
2. **Join the Conversation**:
    - Follow thought leaders of AI ethics and digital rights groups. Engage with content that challenges your assumptions. Vet, verify, and validate everything.
3. **Teach Others**:
    - Share what you have learned with family, friends, coworkers, and your community. Build grassroots literacy programs. Start with a conversation.
4. **Advocate**:
    - AI Advocacy serves as a bridge between AI technology and the broader public, including hospitals, EMR vendors, businesses, developers, policymakers, and communities.
    - Help people to understand and navigate AI's capabilities, limitations, and implications.

CHAPTER FOUR:
Algorithms, Clicks, and Likes

How AI is Shaping Our Digital Desires?

How many times have you seen or heard the word "algorithm" thrown around on social media? It is actually a whole new topic of conversation. I can almost guarantee that, at some point, your favorite YouTuber has complained about, or expressed concern for, pleasing the almighty algorithm.

We live in an era where our decisions—what we watch, what we buy, even what we believe—are increasingly guided by algorithms. Each time we scroll through social media, binge-watch a show, or shop online, we leave behind digital footprints. These footprints fuel the algorithms that shape what we see next.

Clicks, likes, and shares are no longer just digital gestures—they are external validation signals in vast feedback loops powering attention economies. Tech giants have weaponized engagement, using AI-driven algorithms, to predict, influence, and monetize human behavior. This chapter unpacks how algorithms operate behind the scenes, why they matter, and what their influence means for society.

What Is an Algorithm?

We discussed this in the last chapter, but to recap, an **algorithm** is a set of instructions or rules designed to solve a problem or complete a task. In the digital world, algorithms automate decision-making processes. Particularly on social media, you will run into:

- **Sorting Algorithms**
    - Decide what content appears first.
- **Recommendation Algorithms**
    - Suggest videos, products, or news based on previous clicks.
- **Engagement Algorithms**
    - Prioritize content most likely to trigger emotional reactions—whether outrage, laughter, or curiosity.

These invisible systems are not neutral. They are designed with specific goals, often optimized for engagement, ad revenue, or user retention.

The Click Economy—Data is Currency

In the digital marketplace, attention is the most valuable currency. Businesses collect, store, process, and profit from your data, as well as mine. Every click, like, share, or comment fuels revenue generation for the wealthy, using machine learning systems. Here's how the cycle works:

1. **User Behavior**:
    i. You click on a post, like a photo, or watch a video.

2. **Data Collection**:

    ii. Platforms capture and monetize this interaction.

3. **Machine Learning Models**:

    iii. Algorithms analyze your behavior to predict how you will engage.

4. **Content Curation**:

    iv. The platform serves more of what it thinks you will like, to keep you scrolling.

The system creates a **feedback loop** where your preferences are constantly refined, not necessarily for your benefit; the primary goal is always to maximize profits for the platform.

Section 3: The Power of Likes and Shares

A **"like"** might seem trivial, but it represents data that algorithms use to rank and amplify your content. The more interactions a post gets, the more likely it is to be promoted.

This creates phenomena such as:

- **Virality**:
    - Content spreads rapidly when it triggers strong engagement.
- **Echo Chambers**:
    - Algorithms feed users similar content, reinforcing biases.
- **Emotional Hijacking**:
    - Content that provokes anger, fear, or excitement often receives more clicks, regardless of truth, quality, or ethical implications.

Allegedly, platforms like Facebook, Instagram, TikTok, and YouTube prioritize time spent on the platform over accuracy or well-being. The result? Algorithms do not just reflect preferences—they shape them.

The Psychological Impact

Behavioral psychology meets technology in the era of the engagement economy. Social platforms are designed to exploit human vulnerabilities:

- **Dopamine Loops**:
  - Each like or notification triggers a small dopamine release, reinforcing compulsive behavior.
- **FOMO (Fear of Missing Out)**:
  - Algorithmic feeds keep users constantly checking for updates.
- **Social Validation**:
  - The number of likes becomes a proxy for personal worth, driving them to seek external validation, impacting their mental wellbeing.

These systems create addictive cycles, not by accident, but by design.

Ethical and Social Implications

Bias and Manipulation

Algorithms are trained on historical data, which may include biased patterns. As a result, recommendation systems can reinforce harmful stereotypes, spread misinformation, or amplify divisive content.

Surveillance Capitalism

Your clicks and likes are harvested for profit. Let this sink in. If your child has a smartphone, their data is "allegedly" being harvested for profit. These companies collect massive amounts of behavioral data, creating detailed profiles used for targeted advertising, buyer manipulations, and political persuasion.

Loss of Autonomy

When algorithms dictate what you see, they subtly shape your worldview, how you think, what you believe, and the decisions that you make, limiting exposure to diverse ideas or viewpoints.

The Path Forward—Can We Reclaim Control?

Yes, we can. But it won't be easy. We have allowed the Tech Giants to have the controls for a very long time. But, we can demand some sort of legislation that gives us back our autonomy as users, and also educate ourselves about how our data is being used against us and how to stop sharing it. To reduce the negative impact of algorithmic engagement, experts suggest:

- **Algorithmic Transparency**:
    - Companies should disclose how recommendation engines work. Who are the AI Model Trainers? What qualifies them for these roles?
- **Ethical AI Design**:
    - Shift incentives from maximizing engagement to supporting well-being.

- **Digital Literacy**:
    - Educate users on how algorithms influence their behavior.
- **User Control**:
    - Give individuals more power to customize feeds and limit data collection.

Reader Reflection

Without spiraling into much of an existential crisis, here's something you can think about.

1. How much of your digital behavior is truly your choice, and how much is nudged by algorithms?

Reader Strategy | People Powered Intelligence (PPI)

Here's a bit of homework for you from this chapter:

1. Review your social media usage patterns. Are you choosing content, or is it choosing you?
2. Adjust your platform settings to reduce algorithmic influence where possible (turn off autoplay, adjust recommendations, use time limits).
3. Practice "**conscious clicking**"—engage with content intentionally, not impulsively.
4. Stay informed about algorithmic bias and advocate for transparency in tech policies.

CHAPTER FIVE:
How AI is Reshaping Our Daily Lives

"AI is not just a futuristic idea; it's already woven into the fabric of our everyday existence—from how we think, to how we shop, to how we heal."

Welcome to the AI-Infused World

At the risk of sounding like a broken record, Artificial Intelligence is not coming—it is already here. I can't stress that enough. From morning routines powered by intelligent assistants to algorithms that recommend what we watch, buy, and even whom we date, AI is silently integrating into our daily decisions. The more we understand these systems, the better prepared we are to interact with them intelligently, critically, and responsibly.

---

1. AI at Home: The Rise of Smart Living

1. **Smart Assistants**:
   - Devices like Alexa, Google Home, and Siri process voice commands using natural language processing (NLP).
2. **Predictive Convenience**:
   - Smart thermostats, such as Nest, learn from user behavior to conserve energy and reduce costs.

3. **Entertainment Curation**:
    - Platforms like Netflix and Spotify use AI to tailor content based on the types of programs you watch. AI collects data and stores your preferences and habits.

AI makes your life easier, but it does collect your data to do so. Are you aware of what you are trading for that convenience? Is it a fair trade?

---

2. AI at Work: The Evolving Digital Colleague

1. **Productivity Tools**:
    - Microsoft Copilot and Google Workspace utilize AI to automate tasks such as email drafting, summarization, and scheduling.
2. **Hiring & HR**:
    - AI screens resumes, predicts job fit, and even monitors employee sentiment through analytics.
3. **Decision Support**:
    - Executives now rely on AI dashboards that provide predictive insights into customer behavior and market trends.

AI is not replacing the modern workforce—it is being restructured around it.

---

3. AI in Healthcare: Healing Smarter

- **Clinical Decision Support**: Systems analyze thousands of patient records to assist diagnosis and recommend treatments.
- **RCM & Coding Automation**: AI identifies documentation, coding, and billing errors. AI also accelerates the prior authorization process and enhances the quality and accuracy of claims.
- **Wearables & Remote Monitoring**: Devices like Apple Watch or continuous glucose monitors analyze real-time data to flag anomalies.

In medicine, AI is becoming a collaborator.

---

4. AI in Transportation: From Traffic to Tesla

- **Navigation & Traffic**: Google Maps and Waze analyze user data to suggest optimal routes and warn about road conditions.
- **Self-Driving Technology**: Companies like Tesla, Waymo, and Cruise train autonomous systems using reinforcement learning.
- **Public Transit Optimization**: AI helps cities predict demand and optimize routes for buses and ride-sharing systems.

The way we move is evolving—with AI as the silent driver (pun intended).

---

5. AI in Finance & Commerce: Smarter Spending and Saving

- **Fraud Detection**:
  - AI flags unusual transactions with greater speed and accuracy than traditional systems.
- **Personal Finance Assistants**:
  - Tools like Cleo and Mint offer AI-driven budgeting, saving tips, and spending analysis.
- **E-commerce Personalization**:
  - Amazon and Shopify dynamically update product recommendations based on browsing patterns and purchase history.

AI is becoming your personal accountant, with decision-making influence over your financial behavior, by tracking when you spend your money and what you spend it on.

---

6. AI in Education: A Customized Learning Revolution

- **Adaptive Learning Platforms**:
  - Tools like Khan Academy and Coursera personalize content based on performance and learning style.
- **Grading Automation**:
  - AI helps educators with grading essays and short answers, freeing time for student engagement.

- **Skill Forecasting**:
    - Platforms use AI to suggest in-demand skills based on job market data.

The classroom of tomorrow is already here, driven by intelligent feedback loops and personalized curriculum.

---

7. AI and Daily Ethics: Choices, You Do not Know You are Making

- **Data Collection and Consent**:
    - Many AI tools operate in the background, collecting, profiling, and making inferences without explicit consent.
        - **Example:** when working on different projects, I am required to undergo background checks.
        - Two different background checking companies were provided "explicit" seven-year look-back guidelines.
        - Both, without authorization, decided to conduct 0-99 year look-backs.
        - I challenged the results, corrections were made, but it is still unsettling that background checking companies are foregoing authorizations and taking matters into their own hands to extend look-back periods.
- **Algorithmic Bias**:
    - From facial recognition to credit scoring, bias can have real-world consequences.

- **Example:** I applied for a personal loan in 2024. This was the third time that I had done business with this lender.
- They pulled my credit with a particular consumer credit reporting agency.
- For one pull, my credit score dropped 45 points. When five to ten points is the standard for hard pulls.
- Was it the AI, the algorithm, or human error?

- **Surveillance Capitalism**:
    - As AI models profit from personal behavior, questions arise: Who owns your data? How is it being used?
        - What guardrails are in place to protect us?
        - What kind of quality and compliance infrastructure are the leaders of the AI technology implementing to keep us safe?

With every app we use, we leave digital breadcrumbs. AI gathers them and often decides our next move based on them.

Reader Reflection

We are no longer passive consumers in a digital age. As AI becomes more embedded in our lives, we must become more intentional with our interactions. The power of AI lies not just in its complexity, but in how **we choose to use it—or how we allow it to shape us**. Ask yourself:

1. How many of the AI systems discussed are you using daily without even realizing it?

2. In which areas of your life has AI made things better, or more concerning?

Reader Strategy | People Powered Intelligence (PPI)

Here's some homework for you from this chapter:

1. **Audit Your AI Footprint**:
    - Identify the AI-powered tools and services you use on a daily basis.
2. **Ask Questions**:
    - Who owns the data you are sharing? What algorithms are influencing your choices?
3. **Stay Informed**:
    - Read the fine print. Follow reliable AI news sources. Know how to opt in—and how to opt out.
4. **Start Small**:
    - Learn to use an AI tool (like ChatGPT!) with intention, whether for planning, learning, or decision-making.

CHAPTER SIX:
Survive

The Human-AI Power Shift

In the same way electricity redefined labor, AI is redefining *power.* But unlike the machines of the past, this one makes decisions, influences behavior, and adapts faster than most people can understand what is happening. By the time this book is published, AI-powered machines will have advanced beyond what is presented in this version.

This Chapter introduces the "Human-AI Power Shift"—a central theme in this book. Fair warning, a lot of this will sound very scary and concerning. We will examine how AI is subtly yet profoundly altering the flow, control, and authority in our personal, professional, and civic lives. As we journey through this new terrain, we will confront a core question: **Can humans still lead in an AI-powered world, or will we become followers of our own creations?**

I. From Human Judgment to Algorithmic Decision-Making

In workplaces and industries once governed by expert opinions and intuition, AI is increasingly changing the course. We are seeing the focus of authority shift from humans to machines in many domains, even healthcare where stakes are particularly high.

- **Example No. 1:**

  In healthcare, IBM Watson once made treatment recommendations for cancer care based on millions of clinical papers—although ultimately flawed, it revealed how healthcare leadership began to trust AI over even seasoned clinicians [Ross & Swetlitz, 2017].

- **Example No. 2:**

  Some of the end-to-end hiring platforms that utilize filtering tools to identify the most qualified candidates, although beneficial, have reportedly come under scrutiny, with questions raised about how bias and a lack of transparency are impacting machine-made hiring decisions.

As humans increasingly choose to "outsource" decision-making, we risk losing not only control but also an *understanding* of how these decisions are being made. This black-box phenomenon—often referred to as the "automation bias" —is an issue with algorithms that leads to blind trust in AI, even when its output is flawed or ethically questionable [Logg, Minson & Moore, 2019].

- Black box algorithms are computational procedures where the user can only see the inputs and outputs, but not the internal processes or logic that leads to the output.

In other words, black box algorithms are complex systems where the decision-making process is hidden or opaque, making it difficult to understand how a specific result was reached.

II. AI and the Redefinition of Governance

AI has made its way into government procedure as well. Governmental institutions are embracing AI to optimize everything from tax enforcement to policing. But the more governments rely on predictive algorithms, the more they risk entrenching existing inequalities under the guise of objectivity.

- **Predictive Policing:** Tools like Geolitical, also known as PredPol (*until it was rebranded in 2021*), forecast crime hotspots using historical data. However, if the data is biased (*typically referred to as "dirty data"),* the AI may reinforce discriminatory policing patterns [Richardson, Schultz, & Crawford, 2019].
- **Social Credit Systems (SCS):** In China, AI-driven surveillance and scoring systems assign citizens a social rating that affects access to jobs, loans, or travel. This creates a techno-authoritarian feedback loop where power is algorithmically enforced [Creemers, 2018]. Based on violations or low scores, individuals can be black listed.
- **Automated Bureaucracy:** Estonia, widely known as the first "digital nation," is a leader in digital governance that uses AI for tax filings, digital IDs, and even legislation drafting. While efficient, it raises concerns about democratic oversight and due process.

All of this is concerning for many reasons. To start, citizens are being governed by code they don't even necessarily understand, let alone question. Similarly, officials relying on the AI's output might not even have an adequate understanding of how the results were produced, making any biases in the system a complete blind spot. It is almost dystopian.

III. Personal Life: The Subtle Erosion of Autonomy

Consider your Spotify playlists, your Google Maps routes, your TikTok feed—AI is shaping your tastes, travel, and even attention. This convenience masks a profound, philosophical power shift: your choices are no longer entirely your own. And unfortunately, some of us are not paying attention to this power shift. AI is inconspicuously making decisions for you.

- **Example No. 1:**

  Algorithmic Manipulation: Social media algorithms maximize engagement, often by amplifying outrage or misinformation. The 2018 Cambridge Analytica scandal revealed how data was weaponized to influence political opinion without users' awareness [Isaak & Hanna, 2018]. Was 50 million Facebook users' data harvested for Cambridge Analytica?

- **Example No. 2:**

  Predictive Nudges: Behavioral AI now anticipates that some people will buy, watch, or even vote—before they are even conscious of the predictive nudge that is directing their desires. Shoshana Zuboff warns that *the Age of Surveillance Capitalism* can undermine human agency by turning prediction into control [Zuboff, 2019].

- **Example No. 3:**

  AI as Life Partner or Counselor: Now, AI Chatbot Companions are being recommended as a wellness tool option for mental health. With the rise of emotional AI and companion bots, such as Replika or Woebot, which are classified as emotional companions, has anyone addressed who has access to all the information being offloaded to these machines? Are we sharing vulnerabilities that can be packaged and weaponized against us in the future?

IV. The Power Imbalance: Who Controls the AI?

The shift in power and decision-making is not a humans-to-AI shift—it is from the many to the few who *own and design* the AI. Power is now consolidated among the big tech companies and data brokers, who control AI and the algorithms shaping our society.

- **Example No. 1:**

  Design and Ownership: Most powerful AI systems, such as ChatGPT, DeepSeek, Google DeepMind, and Microsoft Copilot, are proprietary. Their training data, logic, and ethical boundaries are kept private and hidden from the public domain.

- **Example No. 2:**

  Data Colonialism: Is it true that Global South nations (allegedly **Latin America, Africa, Asia, and Oceania, as well as Russian Operators)** often provide the data or human labor (e.g., content moderators, click workers) for AI systems designed and profited from in the Global North? If this is true, this asymmetry creates a group of technocratic elites—what some might call "algorithmic overlords"—who are unelected but shape policy, perception, morality, and even societal disturbances.

V. Can the Power Shift Ever Be Re-Balanced?

AI does not have to be a zero-sum game. Thoughtful governance, ethical design, and human-centered Artificial Intelligence Initiatives can restore balance. However, is anyone paying attention to the shift that is occurring? And, what will be the short-term and long-term impact on our society? Or, do they even care?

- **Big Tech's Role**: This topic has more questions than answers. What factors are driving the stagnation of the development and deployment of AI regulatory standards in healthcare? Is Big Tech pushing for regulations or against them? Are your state leaders doing anything to protect you and your data from AI algorithmic overreach? A few efforts that can make a difference are listed below:
    - **Explainable AI (XAI):** Ensure AI decisions can be understood and contested
    - **AI Ethics Frameworks:** Develop ethical principles that emphasize accountability, fairness, and transparency.
    - **Digital Sovereignty:** Countries such as Brazil and the EU are pushing for data localization laws and AI regulations to regain control from Silicon Valley giants. The United States used to be a leader in establishing guardrails for new technologies to ensure people's protection, but, allegedly, this is no longer the case.

Ultimately, power must shift *towards* humanity, not away from it.

The Choice Ahead

AI will not overthrow humans in a cataclysmic revolt. But it may quietly absorb our choices, our agencies, and our freedoms—unless we understand the implications, and remain vigilant.

This is not just a technological transition—it is a civilizational turning point. The power shift is happening. Whether it leads to empowerment or erosion depends not on what AI *can* do, but on what we as humans *choose* to let it do.

The rise of artificial intelligence is proving to be more than just a technological breakthrough. It is a shift in the balance of power between human agency and machine logic. As algorithms reshape and influence our decisions, we are called to confront a defining truth: **those who understand and guide AI will shape the future—AI may shape those who do not**.

The real challenge lies in **reclaiming human purpose within it and remembering the value of our people-powered intelligence (PPI)**. As we move forward, the question is not whether AI will change the world—it already has. The question is: **Will we continue to allow AI to lead, as we follow? Or, will we rise to the occasion of being the leaders that AI and society need us to be?**

A Few Statistics to Pay Attention to: Speed of Technological Advancements

Open-Source Explosion: Open-Source AI models are accelerating global experimentation and application.

Model Scaling: From GPT-2 (2019) to GPT-4 (2023), GPT-4o (2024), and now GPT-5 (2025). AI models have been advancing and enhancing year over year (YoY). AI is being trained to possess exponential comprehension, reasoning, and multimodal abilities (text, images, and audio).

Training Time: What used to take months can now be reduced to weeks, or even days, hours, or minutes, thanks to computational optimization, hardware programming, and advanced training techniques.

Stats: The number of AI-related patents grew from approximately ~20,000 in 2000 to over 250,000 by 2024 (WIPO & Standard AI Index 2024)

Cross-Industry Adoption Rates

Healthcare Revenue Cycle Management (RCM): AI-powered diagnostics, RCM automation, and personalized treatment recommendations are rapidly scaling, with McKinsey Projecting $360 billion+ in value creation by 2030.

Finance:n77% of financial firms, including FinTech, have deployed AI in fraud detection and algorithmic trading (Deloitte, 2023).

Education: AI tutoring and learning platforms have reached millions of students globally since 2020.

Creative Industries: Over 50% of marketers now use AI tools for content creation (Hubspot, 2024)

Workforce Impact & Economic Penetration

Economic Influence: PwC estimates AI could contribute up to $15.7 trillion to the global economy by 2030. So, who are the current and future beneficiaries of these wealth enhancements?

Job Displacement vs. Augmentation: AI is expected to automate up to 40% of tasks across most jobs by 2030 (Goldman Sachs, 2023). AI-driven layoffs are affecting the job market for recent grads (Nolan, 2025).

Reader Reflection

Before moving on, take a moment to reflect on what you have just read.

Where in your life is AI already making decisions for you?

- Whether at work, in your smartphone, shopping cart, your newsfeed, or your navigation app—are you making choices, or are they being made *for* you?

Reader Strategy | People-Powered Intelligence (PPI)

In what ways did this chapter shift how you view power and decision-making in the AI era?

1. Are there moments in your life when you trusted an algorithm over your own instincts?
2. How do you feel about machines playing a role in government, business your healthcare decisions?

Note: *You do not need to write perfect answers—just honest ones.*

Quick Action Step

Select one AI tool or platform that you use frequently. Spend 10 minutes researching how the algorithms make decisions or recommendations for humans.

- Ask yourself: *Am I comfortable with how me, my children, friends or family members are being influenced by AI?*

Exploring why adaptability, digital literacy, and emotional intelligence will be the true markers of human success in the age of AI. Learn how to thrive—not just survive—by upgrading your mindset, not just your skillset.

CHAPTER SEVEN:
AI Knowledge Gaps

Despite the growing prevalence of AI, a significant fraction of the U.S. population remains disconnected from even a basic understanding of what AI is and how it operates. Recent studies reveal that nearly **one-third of American Adults—approximately 70 to 80 million people—lack fundamental AI literacy**.

This knowledge gap is not evenly distributed; it disproportionately affects **older adults, individuals with lower levels of formal education, and residents of rural or underserved regions**. Without targeted education and equitable access to digital resources, millions risk being left behind in an AI-powered world, widening existing social and economic divides. Either way, this percentage hovers around one in three adults.

Approximate Numbers

- U.S. adult population (2025) is approximately **260 million**.
- **30% × 260 million = ~78 million** adults with low AI literacy.

Why This Matters

- Many Americans **use AI in some form daily** without realizing it—typical tech like chatbots, spam filters, recommendation systems, etc.
- Yet a significant portion **is unable to identify or explain** even basic AI features.
- Closing this gap is key for **ethical use**, guarding against misinformation, and preparing for an AI-powered future.

Potential Age Demographics

- **Younger adults (18–29)** demonstrate stronger digital and AI literacy.
    - For instance, approximately 45% of respondents understand how large language models (like ChatGPT) work, compared to only 15% of those aged 65 and above.
- **Older Americans (50+)** often struggle more; recent studies highlight their motivations to learn about AI, as well as their difficulties in starting and grasping the concepts.

Education

- AI Awareness can sometimes correlate with education level, but does not have to with the appropriate training:
    - **Postgraduate degrees**:
        - 53% correctly identify six common AI applications; approximately 14% of adults

with a high school diploma or less can do the same

- Among college graduates, **49%** understand how large language model (LLM) algorithms produce responses, compared to just **17%** of those whose education ended at high school.

Geography

- Adoption of AI tools (e.g., searching for ChatGPT) is higher in **urban, educated, economically advantaged regions**, especially on the **West Coast** (The Emerging AI Divide in the United States)
- Rural, Appalachian, and Gulf states show persistently **lower engagement and awareness**
- Broadband access, critical for AI usage, is uneven: Southern non-metro areas have the lowest connectivity rates, which hinder AI literacy.

Why This Matters

- **Policy and Outreach** efforts must consider this layered divide: older adults, lower-educated, and rural residents need more targeted AI education.
- **Digital Infrastructure Improvements**, especially broadband access in rural areas, can help bridge the geographic literacy gaps.
- **Educational Initiatives**—such as tighter integration of AI in K–12 and college curricula, can help to build foundational knowledge earlier.

Reader Reflection

As we reflect on the realities presented in this chapter, one truth becomes clear: millions of Americans remain unaware of AI's role in shaping their daily lives despite its place in modern society. The gaps highlighted in this chapter risk creating a society where only a portion of the population fully participates in and benefits from the AI revolution, while others are left behind or vulnerable to misinformation and exploitation.

The consequences of this divide go beyond missed opportunities. Without accessible AI education, individuals may unknowingly surrender control of their data, fall prey to algorithmic bias, or face employment disruptions without the skills to adapt. Closing this gap is not merely to impart technological fluency—it is to **empower individuals to make informed decisions, participate in governance, and thrive in an AI-driven world**.

Reader Strategy | People Powered Intelligence (PPI)

How to Rise, Survive, and Thrive with AI Literacy

Here is your personal strategy to help you move from awareness to action:

1. Assess Your Own AI Literacy

- Take inventory of your current knowledge. Can you explain what AI is? Do you know where you encounter AI daily?
- Use simple online quizzes or AI literacy toolkits to benchmark yourself.

2. Become an AI Explorer, Not a Bystander

- **Engage**: Try out different tools to experience AI—a chatbot, an image generator, or a healthcare portal recommendation engine.
- **Question**: Ask, *"How does this tool work? What data does it use? Who controls it?"*

3. Advocate for Inclusive AI Education

- Support AI literacy programs in your community, especially for **older adults, under-resourced schools, and rural areas**.
- Encourage local libraries, schools, and workforce centers to host AI awareness workshops.

4. Stay Curious and Connected

- Follow AI developments from trusted sources—not just bloggers, or media headlines, but in-depth guides and explainers.
- Join community discussions, webinars, or forums that break down complex AI topics into human terms.

5. Prepare for the Next Chapter

In the chapters ahead, we will explore the distinction between Automation vs. Augmentation, **how to use AI responsibly, avoid digital exploitation, and harness AI for personal and professional growth**. Your role as an informed citizen starts now.

CHAPTER EIGHT:

Automation vs. Augmentation

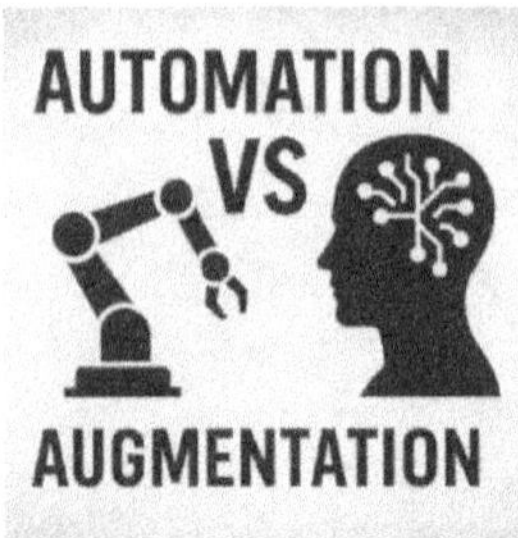

The Battle for the Future of Human Work

"The real question is not whether machines think but whether humans still do." — B.F. Skinner

As businesses, governments, and everyday citizens adopt AI, one vital question is always at the forefront: will AI Automation **replace** us, or will it **empower** us?

For most people, it is not even a question. It is a deep-rooted fear. But a perspective shift might alleviate their concerns while presenting new opportunities.

This debate boils down to two competing paradigms: **automation** vs. **augmentation**.

Understanding the Terms

- **Automation** refers to the complete replacement of human tasks with machines or algorithms. It aims to increase efficiency by removing the need for human intervention.
    - Examples include self-checkout kiosks, robotic assembly lines, and AI-driven claim adjudication systems in the healthcare industry.
- **Augmentation**, by contrast, enhances human capabilities through technology. It keeps the human "in

the loop" using AI to aid in decision-making, speed, or accuracy (Wilson & Daugherty, 2018). Think of an AI-powered clinical decision support system that helps a doctor diagnose rare diseases faster, but does not make the diagnosis alone.

Historical Roots of the Debate

Since the first Industrial Revolution, concerns about machines replacing humans have arisen with each wave of innovation, from the steam engine to the personal computer. But each era also brought new opportunities. The ATM, for instance, was expected to eliminate bank teller jobs. Instead, it allowed tellers to focus on customer service, while banks expanded to more locations.

Today, we are at a similar crossroads.

The Case for Automation

Automation's Appeal is clear:

- **Efficiency & Speed**: Automated systems can handle repetitive tasks faster and without fatigue.
- **Cost Savings**: Reduced labor costs and error rates lead to increased profitability.
- **Scalability**: AI systems can process thousands—or millions—of transactions without requiring more employees.

These benefits have driven automation across various industries, from manufacturing to customer service. In healthcare, for example, AI is automating tasks such as repetitive documentation reviews, medical coding, medical billing, radiology scans, and insurance authorizations. In finance, robo-advisors manage portfolios with no human intervention.

However, a price will be paid at some point.

The Human Toll

A 2023 report by McKinsey estimates that 400–800 million jobs could be displaced by automation by 2030 (McKinsey Global Institute, 2023). Jobs that are routine and predictable, such as data entry clerks, telemarketers, and even paralegals, are most vulnerable.

Worse, automation risks **deskilling** human labor. As algorithms take over decision-making, there is a danger that humans will forget how to think critically or creatively, relying blindly on AI outputs. This will be a big mistake! One of the greatest gifts as humans is our ability to be critical thinkers. Our ability to skillfully analyze, evaluate, and interpret information and make complex decisions using reasoned judgment. These skills are unmatched.

The Promise of Augmentation

Where automation focuses on **replacement**, augmentation seeks **collaboration and partnership**.

AI is particularly powerful when paired with human strengths like:

- **Critical thinking**
- **Domain expertise**
- **Contextual reasoning**
- **Creative problem-solving**

- **Empathy and Ethics**

Consider Radiologists:

An AI may flag suspicious lesions on scans with high precision. However, it is the human doctor who understands the patient's history, weighs competing diagnoses, and discusses treatment options in a compassionate and empathetic manner.

In law, AI tools can analyze contracts and predict case outcomes; however, lawyers still negotiate settlements, build arguments, and present their cases to juries. In business, augmented analytics enables executives to make better decisions by uncovering patterns—without compromising their strategic insight.

This model of "**collaborative intelligence**" is at the heart of augmentation (Daugherty & Wilson, 2018). Organizations that embrace augmentation do not just preserve jobs—they transform them.

Human-AI Synergy: A Strategic Advantage

Augmented intelligence is not just good ethics—it's smart business. A 2021 Harvard Business Review study found that companies combining AI with human expertise outperformed those using AI or humans alone in both productivity and innovation (Ransbotham et al., 2021).

Plus, augmented systems can reduce AI bias. When humans remain involved, they can identify context-specific errors, question odd results, and ensure fairness. As we have seen in medical and criminal justice applications, AI's objectivity can fail when trained on biased data sets (O'Neil, 2016).

Striking the Right Balance

Sure, AI may replace some jobs. But it also creates a whole range of new ones. To survive—and thrive—in an AI-powered world, individuals and organizations must stop asking **"Will AI take my job?"** and start asking **How can AI help to advance my career?**

This requires:

- **Upskilling**:
  - Workers must develop digital fluency, emotional intelligence, and cross-domain knowledge.
- **Redesigning work**:
  - Leaders must restructure roles to promote AI-human collaboration to get the best of both worlds.
- **Ethical frameworks**:
  - Policymakers must guide the development of automation toward social good, not just economic gain.

When done right, AI does not diminish human relevance—it **redefines** it.

Choose To Be on the Right Side of the Future

Automation and augmentation are not mutually exclusive—they are applications of tools. The danger lies not in AI itself, but in how we choose to apply it. The world does not need fewer humans. It needs **smarter, more empowered humans** working alongside machines that enhance our strengths and mitigate our weaknesses.

The future is not man versus machine. It is man **and** machine.

The choice between automation and augmentation is just as much a philosophical decision as a technical one. It will define the kind of society we build, the dignity we preserve, and the work we choose to value.

Choose wisely.

The Battle for the Future of Human Work

Reader Reflection

This chapter challenges the conventional fear of job loss due to artificial intelligence by reframing the conversation: not as "man vs. machine," but as "man with machine." The distinction between automation (replacement) and augmentation (enhancement) is more than semantics—it is strategic. You have seen how automation can lead to increased efficiency, but also displace human jobs. In contrast, augmentation creates job opportunities that foster human growth, creativity, and relevance.

As you reflect, ask yourself:

- In my profession or business, where is automation creeping in—and what impact is it having?
- Where can I personally or organizationally *choose* augmentation instead of replacement?
- What does meaningful work look like in an AI-augmented world?

Remember: Survival in this AI age is not about being irreplaceable by technology—it is about being irreplaceable **with** it.

Reader Strategy | People Powered Intelligence (PPI)

1. Identify Your Role in the Shift

Make a list of your current job, projects, and tasks. Label which could be automated and which requires human judgment, interaction, collaboration, empathy, or creativity. This awareness is your blueprint for future-proofing your career.

2. Focus on Human Strengths

Invest in skills AI cannot easily replicate—emotional intelligence, strategic thinking, creative thinking, ethical judgment, and cross-disciplinary knowledge. These will be your strongest differentiators.

3. Embrace Collaborative Intelligence

Seek tools that augment your work. Whether you are a healthcare provider, business leader, teacher, medical coder, or auditor, there is likely an AI-powered solution that can elevate your performance. Learn it, use it, improve it, and move it as a revenue-producing skill.

4. Lead the Ethical Conversation

Be the advocate leader in your organization, industry, or friend group for responsible AI use. Ensure that humans stay informed and are looped in on high-stakes decisions. Ask tough questions about fairness, accountability, and transparency.

5. Reframe the Fear

Instead of asking "Will AI take my job?" reframe your mindset:

"How can I become more valuable by working alongside AI?" This single shift in perspective turns fear into opportunity.

In the next chapter, we will explore how humans must upskill and reimagine their place in an AI-powered world—because thriving in this new era will require not just tools, but transformation.

CHAPTER NINE:
Mastering AI Skill Acquisition

The Urgency of AI Fluency

In every era, the workforce has had to adapt to technological shifts. From the steam engine to the internet, those who learned the new tools rose; those who resisted were left behind. Today, the technological disruptor—**Artificial Intelligence**—is rewriting the rules of productivity, decision-making, and innovation at lightning speed.

To rise, survive, and thrive in this new AI-powered world and economy, individuals and organizations must commit to **AI skill acquisition** as a continuous, strategic journey, not a one-time event. To stay ahead and avoid being left behind, you need to steer your career in the direction of AI upskilling or reskilling.

Section 1: The New Literacy—What Are AI Skills?

AI skills extend beyond coding or data science. They encompass a spectrum of competencies that enable individuals to:

- **Understand AI Fundamentals**
  Know the basics of machine learning, natural language processing, computer vision, neural networks, generative AI, and large language models.

- **Interpret and Work with AI Systems**
  Utilize AI tools, such as chatbots, AI-driven analytics, and automation software, effectively, which help you perform repetitive daily tasks.
- **Critical AI Literacy**
  Understand AI's capabilities, limitations, and potential biases. Be able to ask: "Is this AI decision transparent, ethical, and fair?"
- **Data Fluency**
  Since AI learns from data, understanding data quality, management, and privacy is essential.
- **Ethics and Governance Awareness**
  Learn how to navigate AI compliance, responsible AI usage, and regulatory requirements.
- **Prompt Engineering and Collaboration with AI**
  Master the art of crafting effective AI prompts to get better outputs from generative tools.

AI skills are not just technical—they are strategic, operational, and ethical.
Everyone from CEOs to front-line staff must become AI-literate to remain relevant.

Section 2: How AI Changes Skill Acquisition—The Evolution of Learning

AI is not just something you learn—it is also something you can learn **with**. The process of skill acquisition itself is being transformed by AI:

- **Personalized Learning Paths**
  AI-driven platforms, such as adaptive learning systems, adjust to your pace, preferences, and knowledge gaps.

- **Microlearning and On-Demand Training**
  Bite-sized lessons, simulations, and interactive AI tutors are making skill-building more accessible than ever before.
- **Real-Time Feedback Loops**
  AI provides immediate feedback, helping learners course-correct on the spot rather than waiting for annual reviews or certifications.
- **Simulation and Virtual Reality Training**
  AI-enhanced simulations create safe environments for practicing complex tasks, like medical procedures, negotiations, or coding sprints.

Section 3: The AI Skill Acquisition Framework

To build AI skills, follow this strategic five-phase framework:

Phase 1: Awareness

Understand what AI is, what it is not, and how it's reshaping industries. This is the "Why AI?" stage.

Phase 2: Assessment

Audit your current skillset. What do you already know? Where are your gaps in technical, ethical, and operational AI understanding?

Phase 3: Acquisition

Start learning through curated courses, AI tools, mentorship, and hands-on experimentation. Utilize platforms such as Coursera, edX, LinkedIn Learning, and AI boot camps.

Phase 4: Application

Apply new skills in real-world projects. Use AI tools in your work or build prototypes. Learning sticks when you **do**.

Phase 5: Advancement

AI evolves rapidly. Keep up with the changes by engaging in discussions and being a part of the conversations. Commit to lifelong learning through continuous upskilling, peer networking, and staying informed on AI developments.

Section 4: Top AI Skills in Demand Today

Here is a snapshot of high-value AI-related skills across industries:

Skill	Description	Applicability
Prompt Engineering	Crafting effective prompts for generative AI tools	Marketing, Writing, Healthcare
Data Analysis & Visualization	Understanding data patterns via AI tools	Business, Finance, Healthcare
Machine Learning Fundamentals	Basics of supervised/unsupervised learning	Tech, Product Development
AI Ethics & Compliance	Navigating ethical and legal AI use	Governance, Compliance

Skill	Description	Applicability
AI-Enhanced Decision-Making	Using AI outputs to inform strategy	Leadership, Operations
Cybersecurity for AI	Securing AI systems against risks	IT, Healthcare, Defense
Automation Workflow Design	Implementing AI automation in processes	RCM, Healthcare, Manufacturing
CDI Automation	Epic AI/ML-Based CDI Assistant	RCM, Clinical Documentation Integrity
Charge Correction & Automation Rules	Review Charges/Modifiers	RCM, Medical Coding

---

Section 5: Barriers to AI Skill Acquisition | How to Overcome Them

Barrier 1: Fear of Technology
Solution: Shift from fear to curiosity. Engage in AI literacy workshops or entry-level courses.

Barrier 2: Lack of Time
Solution: Use microlearning—15-minute daily AI learning sessions can create mastery over time.

Barrier 3: Overwhelming Complexity
Solution: Start small. Focus on practical AI tools before diving into theory-heavy concepts.

Barrier 4: Ethical Concerns and Mistrust
Solution: Study AI ethics concurrently with technical learning to develop a balanced understanding.

Becoming AI Agile

AI skill acquisition is not optional—it is a matter of survival. But it is also an invitation to participate in one of the most exciting technological shifts in human history. Those who invest in AI literacy will become not just consumers of AI but **architects of the future**.

By embracing continuous AI skill development, you will unlock new career pathways, contribute to responsible innovation, and position yourself at the forefront of the next industrial revolution.

The future belongs to the AI-ready. Are you ready to rise to the challenge?

CHAPTER TEN:

The Misinformation About AI Replacing Human Jobs

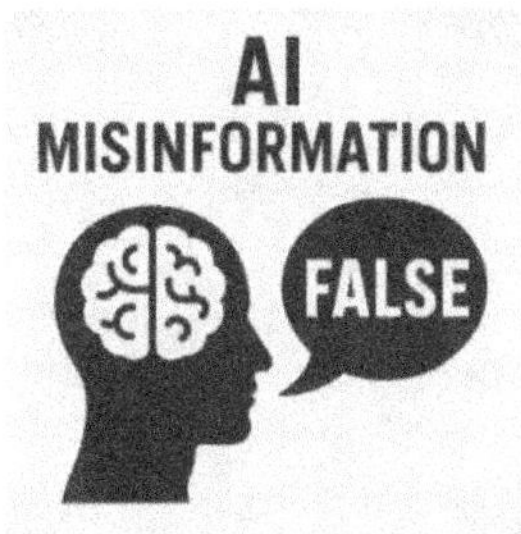

A Reality Check

In the global conversation about Artificial Intelligence, one narrative dominates headlines and social media feeds: **"AI is going to replace all, or most of the human jobs."**

While this statement grabs attention, it is a **misleading oversimplification** of a much more complex reality.

The Truth Behind the Fear

There is no denying that AI and automation are transforming the workforce. Routine, repetitive, and rule-based tasks are being automated at a rapid pace. However, the widespread fear that **AI will replace humans in every job category** is **rooted in sensationalism, misunderstanding, and—most importantly—fear**.

Most experts agree that **AI is more likely to augment human roles rather than eliminate them**, especially in jobs that require human judgment, creativity, empathy, or hands-on skills.

The conversation needs to shift from AI **"job replacement"** to AI **"job redefinition."**

Jobs AI Will Not Be Able to Replace

1. Healthcare & Human Care Roles

- Nurses & Nurse Practitioners
- Doctors (particularly in surgery, diagnostics, and patient care)
- Psychiatrists, Psychologists, and Therapists
- Physical & Occupational Therapists
- Home Health Aides & Caregivers
- Midwives & OB-GYNs
- Hospice Workers
- Veterinarians & Veterinary Technicians

2. Creative & Artistic Professions

- Writers (Literary Fiction, Memoir, Philosophy, Poetry)
- Screenwriters & Playwrights
- Visual Artists (Painters, Sculptors, Installations)
- Musicians, Composers, & Performers
- Fashion Designers & Haute Couture Creators
- Culinary Chefs (Creative & Experiential Dining)

3. Leadership & Decision-Making Roles

- CEOs & Strategic Business Leaders
- Political Leaders & Diplomats
- Judges & Ethics Boards (Moral Reasoning & Contextual Decisions)
- Crisis Managers & Emergency Coordinators

4. Education & Mentorship

- Teachers & Early Childhood Educators (Especially Pre-K to Elementary)
- Life Coaches & Personal Development Mentors
- Special Education Instructors
- Spiritual Leaders & Pastors

5. Skilled Trades & Craftsmanship

- Electricians & Plumbers (On-Site Problem Solving)
- Construction Workers & Master Carpenters
- Custom Furniture Makers & Woodworkers
- Auto Mechanics & Repair Technicians (Complex Diagnostics in Physical Spaces)

6. Social & Emotional Support Roles

- Social Workers & Case Managers
- Conflict Mediators & Negotiators
- Community Organizers & Grassroots Leaders

7. Safety, Security & Emergency Response

- Firefighters
- Paramedics & EMTs
- Police Officers (Especially Community-Based Policing)
- Disaster Relief Coordinators

8. Ethics, Philosophy, and Human Wisdom

- Ethicists & Moral Philosophers
- Clergy & Religious Leaders

- Cultural Anthropologists & Historians
- AI & Algorithm Auditors (Ensuring AI Compliance & Integrity)

9. Human Experience & Emotional Connection Jobs

- Actors & Performers (Theater, Film, Live Performance)
- Event Planners (Weddings, Cultural Ceremonies)
- Tour Guides (Experiential Storytelling)
- Counselors & Peer Support Specialists

Why These Jobs Are AI-Resistant:

Reason	Explanation
Empathy & Compassion	AI lacks true emotional intelligence and is unable to establish trust or form a deep human connection. AI has IQ but not EQ.
Creativity & Original Thought	AI can assist in creation, but cannot replicate the raw, novel, or avant-garde imagination of humans.
Complex Physical Interaction	Many jobs involve unpredictable environments that require human dexterity and perception.
Ethics & Moral Judgment	AI cannot make nuanced ethical decisions or understand cultural and situational morality.

Reason	Explanation
Human Experience	Roles that require shared life experiences, cultural understanding, and storytelling are inherently human.

Why the Misinformation Spreads

Source of Misinformation	Explanation
Media Sensationalism	Headlines prioritize fear-based clickbait, focusing on "job loss" over "job evolution."
Tech Industry Hype	Some tech leaders exaggerate AI's capabilities to attract funding or attention.
Misunderstanding AI's Limits	Many people conflate *narrow AI* (task-specific) with *general AI* (human-level). We do not yet have true general AI.
Historical Technophobia	Each technological revolution, from the steam engine to the internet, sparked fears of mass unemployment that never fully materialized.

Jobs Will Evolve, Not Vanish

- **AI will replace tasks, not entire professions.**
- New roles will emerge in AI development, management, oversight, compliance, and ethics.

- Human skills, such as critical thinking, relationship building, emotional intelligence, and creativity, will become **increasingly valuable, not less so**.

The Real Risks of Misinformation

The danger of this false narrative is twofold:

1. **Workforce Paralysis**
    - People may feel hopeless, fearing inevitable job loss rather than preparing for new opportunities.
2. **Policy Missteps**
    - Federal, State, and Local Governments; large, medium, and small organizations may overreact or underinvest in **upskilling programs.**

AI is not the end of human work; it is the beginning of a new era of collaborative partnership between humans and machines.

The key is to become laser-focused on **adapting, upskilling, and redefining roles**, not surrendering to fear.

CHAPTER ELEVEN

Survival of the Smartest, or the Strongest

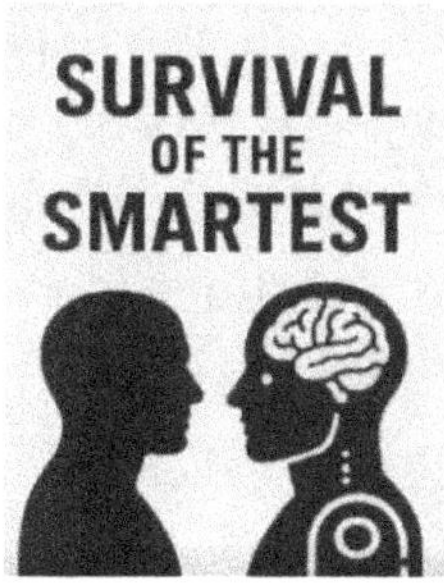

Why Adaptability? Digital Literacy and Emotional Intelligence Will Define Human Relevance in an AI-Dominated Future.

"It is not the strongest of the species that survives, nor the most intelligent, but the one most adaptable to change."

— **Charles Darwin** *(attributed)*

I. The Intelligence Shift is Underway

For most of human history, survival has favored those with physical strength. Then, with the industrial and information revolutions, intelligence took the precedence. Now, in the age of artificial intelligence (AI), even raw cognitive power is being challenged by machines that can outperform humans in analysis, prediction, and in some cases, creativity.

In some ways, if you really oversimplify the AI controversy, it seems like human evolution is regressing.

However, while AI is accelerating in speed and scope, it lacks what humans must now double down on: adaptability, ethical reasoning, and emotional connection.

II. The New Standard of Strength

In a world increasingly shaped by artificial intelligence, the notion of being able to survive life's most challenging times is rapidly moving away from physical prowess or sheer intellect. Instead, it hinges on adaptability—the ability to evolve in response to rapid technological shifts. The age-old notion that the "fittest" are the strongest is losing its grip. In the AI era, survival favors those who are emotionally intelligent, digitally literate, and capable of continuous reinvention.

III. Adaptability: The Core of Human Evolution

The pace of technological change is accelerating at a rate that exceeds linear human comprehension. According to a 2023 report by the **World Economic Forum (WEF)**, nearly 44% of workers' core skills are expected to change within five years. Jobs are evolving, vanishing, or being repurposed—sometimes overnight.

This AI era favors individuals who:

- See change as a feature, not an inconvenience.
- Continuously learn and unlearn.
- Apply human judgment in real-time to the shifting environment.

Case Study:

During the COVID-19 pandemic, companies and workers who quickly adapted to virtual platforms, automated workflows, and AI-enhanced services not only survived—they often outperformed traditional players (McKinsey & Company, 2021).

AI systems can outpace human minds in milliseconds, analyze petabytes of data, and automate once-coveted white-collar roles. However, they lack one crucial trait: the human capacity for contextual reinvention. The World Economic

Forum (2023) identifies **resilience and adaptability** as core 21st-century skills, essential for surviving and thriving in volatile, AI-transformed economies.

Companies that adopted remote work, AI integration, and platform-based services during the COVID-19 pandemic made it through and thrived. So much so that most of them have gone permanently remote.

Similarly, individuals who transitioned from traditional roles to hybrid digital capacities have redefined job security on their own terms.

IV. Digital Literacy: The New Global Language

Just as reading and writing became essential in the print era, **digital literacy** is the new baseline for economic participation. According to the Organization for Economic Co-operation and Development **(OECD) program for the International Assessment of Adult Competencies (PIAAC)**, individuals with strong digital problem-solving skills are significantly more likely to participate in the labor force and earn higher wages.

Digital Literacy Includes:

- Understanding AI and algorithmic systems.
- Navigating data privacy, quality, and compliance
- Evaluating online information critically.
- Collaborating across tech-enhanced environments.

Without these skills, individuals risk becoming **digitally invisible** and economically disadvantaged.

Digital ignorance today is akin to **functional illiteracy** in the industrial age. **Emotional Intelligence is Humanity's Differentiator.** AI can detect sentiment and even simulate empathy. But it cannot **authentically** experience emotions or ethically navigate the complexities of human relationships.

Emotional Intelligence (EI) is our superpower. EI is our ability to recognize, understand, and manage emotions, which gives us, humans, a distinct advantage over the rise of AI and immunizes us from being displaced by it.

According to a McKinsey Global Institute study (2022), **roles requiring social and emotional skills are among the least susceptible to automation**. Leaders, caregivers, mentors, mediators, and creative professionals who master emotional intelligence (EI) will continue to play irreplaceable roles in AI-rich societies.

EI Will also play a Crucial Role In:

- **Collaborative Innovation**, where human teams co-create with AI systems;
- **Ethical Decision-Making**, where AI recommendations must be reviewed, evaluated, and filtered through human judgment;
- **Social Resilience**, where communities must heal to survive the devastation of job displacements and digital divides.

V. The Rise of the Human-AI Hybrid

The future of work and life is **hybrid**. Not just remote or in-office, but **humans + machines**. Those who will rise, survive, and thrive are not necessarily the ones with the most credentials or intelligence, but those who can **partner with AI to amplify their strengths** and **navigate change without losing their core identity**.

This hybridization requires:

- **Lifelong Learning Mindsets**—not degrees, but upskilling cycles;

- **Growth-Oriented Adaptability**—treating disruption as an opportunity;
- **Cross-Functional Agility**—combining soft skills with tech fluency.

Evolve or Fade

In this AI-dominated world, **brute strength** will prove to be irrelevant. Static knowledge will seem outdated quickly. The torch of relevance passes to those who can **dance with disruption**. The smartest are those who understand AI, themselves, others, and what the future is calling for us to know: how to utilize AI, and how to prepare, rise, and thrive in partnership with machines.

Societies and Survival now lean towards favoring the **curious**, the **compassionate**, and the **digitally empowered**.

Reader Reflection

As you close out the final chapter of this book, consider the **paradigm shift** we explored: survival in the age of AI will no longer be determined by **brute strength** or even traditional intellect alone. The most successful individuals and organizations will be those who embrace **adaptability**, invest in **digital literacy**, and cultivate **emotional intelligence**.

Ask yourself:

- Do I understand how AI is impacting my profession and daily life?
- Am I growing not only in technical knowledge, but in self-awareness and interpersonal skills?

Your relevance in an AI-driven world does not depend on becoming more like machines—it depends on becoming **more human** than ever before.

Reader Strategy | People Powered Intelligence (PPI)

Here is how you, as a reader and future-forward thinker, should begin to take action:

1. Audit Your Adaptability

- Reflect on how you typically respond to change. Ask: *Do I resist, react, reframe, or retrain to align with changes?*
- Start a monthly habit of embracing a new technology, workflow, or perspective.

Try This: Keep a "Disruption Journal" to track how you adapt and what you learn from each shift.

2. Boost Your Digital Literacy

- Learn the basics of AI algorithms, automation, and data privacy.
- Explore how digital tools are changing your industry or profession.

Action Step: Commit to completing one free online course in digital skills or AI literacy this year.

CONCLUSION:
What Do We Do Now?

We stand at a turning point unlike any in human history. Artificial Intelligence (AI) is doing more than just changing industries—it is redefining what it means to be human in the 21st century. From healthcare to finance, education to entertainment, AI is rapidly becoming the silent partner that shapes our decisions, influences our economies, and transforms our daily lives.

Yet the future remains uncertain and unwritten.

The central question is not whether AI will dominate the world, but how humans will choose to participate in this transformation. Will we passively react, falling victim to disruption and misinformation, playing out the dystopian trope we see in movies? Or will we tap into our people-powered intelligence (PPI) and use it to enthusiastically rise, survive, and thrive with AI by embracing new skills, fostering emotional intelligence, and asserting our ethical leadership?

AI systems are mimicking human cognitive functions—learning from data, adapting to new inputs, and continuously using this data to optimize its performance over time. **Adaptability is now considered the currency of survival.** Digital literacy is no longer optional—it is the new standard for relevance. Emotional intelligence and our PPI remain our most valuable assets in an increasingly algorithm-driven world.

The next era of progress will not be led solely by machines. It will be led by humans who are wise enough to collaborate with AI without losing our humanity—individuals and organizations who know when to accelerate innovation and when to pause for ethical reflection. We owe it to ourselves to catch up and keep up.

The future belongs to the builders, the learners, the ethical leaders, and the curious minds who are ready to rise with AI, not be replaced by it.

> This is our moment.
> Not to fear AI, but to understand it.
> Not to resist change, but to guide it.
> Not to survive by default, but to thrive by design.

The AI revolution is here. **Now it is our turn to decide** if we will rise to the occasion, survive the disruption, and thrive beyond our wildest dreams **of leading with** and the boundaries of change!

APPENDIX I

AI & OG Decree

For Older Generations, By Older Generations, With Artificial Intelligence (AI)

Article I | Recognition of Legacy

We affirm that our values do not fade with time, nor do our contributions expire. Our history and wisdom help to form the foundation upon which new technologies are built. AI may calculate, but it cannot replicate our lived truth.

Article II | Commitment to Adaptation

We shall rise with courage, learning and adapting to the tools of Artificial Intelligence, not as bystanders but as participants, inventors, and leaders. We will not be left behind. We claim our seat at the digital table, equipped with curiosity, information, and determination.

Article III | Survival Through Wisdom

Our assets are not only in surviving the AI Revolution, but in guiding others. We will use our judgment, perspective, and people-powered intelligence (PPI) to ensure AI serves humanity, not the other way around. Rising and surviving for us means steering technology with ethics, compassion, and common sense.

Article IV | Thriving in the New Age

We will thrive by blending experience with innovation. We choose empowerment over fear, inclusion over isolation, and growth over stagnation. AI is not here to replace us-it is here to amplify our voices, extend our reach, and carry our new legacies forward.

Article V | Declaration of Rights

- We have the right to AI education that is simple, accessible, and respectful of our pace.
- We have the right to AI tools that enhance our independence, not diminish it.
- We have the right to equity in the AI economy, ensuring that older generations are beneficiaries, not casualties, of progress.
- We have the right to dignity, always. Technology must serve us, never strip us of respect.

Final Oath

We, the OGs, stand united-not as relics of the past but as torchbearers for the future. With Artificial Intelligence by our side, we will rise above doubt, survive the change, and thrive in the new age.

So decreed. So honored. So lived.

Corliss Collins

Elder Signature/Leader/Mentor/Coach

APPENDIX II

This is a list of exceptional resources that were used as a reference to help enhance and expand on the knowledge and understanding of Artificial Intelligence:

Chapter One: Introduction

Mayor, A. (2018). *Gods and robots: Myths, machines, and ancient dreams of technology*. Princeton University Press.

Needham, J. (1986). *Science and civilization in China: Volume 2, History of scientific thought*. Cambridge University Press.

Al-Jazari. (1206). *The book of knowledge of ingenious mechanical devices.* (Various translations available).

Descartes, R. (1637). *Discourse on the method*. Project Gutenberg. https://www.gutenberg.org/ebooks/59

Leibniz, G. W. (1686). *The discourse on metaphysics* and *The monadology*. (Public domain translations available).

Boole, G. (1854). *An investigation of the laws of thought*. Project Gutenberg. https://www.gutenberg.org/ebooks/15114

Turing, A. M. (1936). On computable numbers, with an application to the Entscheidungsproblem. *Proceedings of the London Mathematical Society*, *s2–42*(1), 230–265. https://doi.org/10.1112/plms/s2-42.1.230

Turing, A. M. (1950). Computing machinery and intelligence. *Mind*, *59*(236), 433–460. https://doi.org/10.1093/mind/LIX.236.433

McCarthy, J., Minsky, M., Rochester, N., & Shannon, C. (1955). *A proposal for the Dartmouth summer research project on artificial intelligence*. http://www-formal.stanford.edu/jmc/history/dartmouth/dartmouth.html

Weizenbaum, J. (1966). ELIZA—A computer program for the study of natural language communication between man and machine. *Communications of the ACM*, *9*(1), 36–45. https://doi.org/10.1145/365153.365168

Crevier, D. (1993). *AI: The tumultuous history of the search for artificial intelligence*. Basic Books.

Newell, A., & Simon, H. A. (1956). *The logic theorist*. (Technical Report, RAND Corporation).

Dreyfus, H. L. (1972). *What computers can't do: A critique of artificial reason*. MIT Press.

Russell, S., & Norvig, P. (2021). *Artificial intelligence: A modern approach* (4th ed.). Pearson.

Krizhevsky, A., Sutskever, I., & Hinton, G. E. (2012). ImageNet classification with deep convolutional neural networks. *Advances in Neural Information Processing Systems*, *25*, 1097–1105. https://papers.nips.cc/paper/2012/hash/c399862d3b9d6b76c8436e924a68c45b-Abstract.html

Silver, D., Huang, A., Maddison, C. J., et al. (2016). Mastering the game of Go with deep neural networks and tree search. *Nature*, *529*(7587), 484–489. https://doi.org/10.1038/nature1696

Brown, T., Mann, B., Ryder, N., et al. (2020). Language models are few-shot learners. *arXiv preprint arXiv:2005.14165*. https://arxiv.org/abs/2005.14165

OpenAI. (2023). *GPT-4 technical report*. https://cdn.openai.com/papers/gpt-4.pdf

European Commission. (2021). *Proposal for a regulation on artificial intelligence (AI Act).* https://ec.europa.eu/info/sites/default/files/commission-proposal-regulation-artificial-intelligence-april2021_en.pdf

The White House. (2023, October 30). *Executive order on the safe, secure, and trustworthy development and use of artificial intelligence.* https://www.whitehouse.gov/briefing-room/presidential-actions/2023/10/30/executive-order-on-safe-secure-and-trustworthy-artificial-intelligence/

OECD. (2019). *OECD principles on artificial intelligence.* https://oecd.ai/en/ai-principles

Chapter Two: Rise with AI

Brynjolfsson, E., & McAfee, A. (2014). *The second machine age: Work, progress, and prosperity in a time of brilliant technologies.* W. W. Norton & Company.

Bughin, J., Hazan, E., Ramaswamy, S., Chui, M., Allas, T., Dahlström, P., Henke, N., & Trench, M. (2018). *Skill shift: Automation and the future of the workforce.* McKinsey Global Institute. https://www.mckinsey.com/featured-insights/future-of-work/skill-shift-automation-and-the-future-of-the-workforce

Coursera. (n.d.). *AI for everyone.* Coursera. https://www.coursera.org/learn/ai-for-everyone

Davenport, T. H., & Ronanki, R. (2018). Artificial intelligence for the real world. *Harvard Business Review*, *96*(1), 108–116. https://hbr.org/2018/01/artificial-intelligence-for-the-real-world

Floridi, L., Cowls, J., Beltrametti, M., Chatila, R., Chazerand, P., Dignum, V., … & Vayena, E. (2018). AI4People—An ethical framework for a good AI society: Opportunities, risks, principles, and recommendations. *Minds and Machines, 28*(4), 689–707. https://doi.org/10.1007/s11023-018-9482-5

Google AI. (n.d.). *Learn with Google AI.* Google. https://ai.google/education/

Haenlein, M., Kaplan, A., Tan, C.-W., & Zhang, P. (2022). Artificial intelligence (AI) in business and management: State of the art and research agenda. *Journal of Business Research, 145*, 926–940. https://doi.org/10.1016/j.jbusres.2022.03.027

Topol, E. (2019). *Deep medicine: How artificial intelligence can make healthcare human again.* Basic Books.

Wilson, H. J., Daugherty, P. R., & Davenport, T. H. (2019). The future of work: How artificial intelligence will transform the employee experience. *MIT Sloan Management Review.* https://sloanreview.mit.edu/article/the-future-of-work-how-ai-will-transform-the-employee-experience/

World Economic Forum. (2020). *Jobs of tomorrow: Mapping opportunity in the new economy.* https://www.weforum.org/reports/jobs-of-tomorrow

Chapter Three: What is AI Literacy?

Brynjolfsson, E., & McAfee, A. (2014). *The second machine age: Work, progress, and prosperity in a time of brilliant technologies.* W. W. Norton & Company.

Bughin, J., Hazan, E., Ramaswamy, S., Chui, M., Allas, T., Dahlström, P., Henke, N., & Trench, M. (2018). *Skill shift: Automation and the future of the workforce.* McKinsey Global Institute. https://www.mckinsey.com/featured-insights/future-of-work/skill-shift-automation-and-the-future-of-the-workforce

Davenport, T. H., & Ronanki, R. (2018). Artificial intelligence for the real world. *Harvard Business Review*, *96*(1), 108–116. https://hbr.org/2018/01/artificial-intelligence-for-the-real-world

Floridi, L., Cowls, J., Beltrametti, M., Chatila, R., Chazerand, P., Dignum, V., … & Vayena, E. (2018). AI4People—An ethical framework for a good AI society: Opportunities, risks, principles, and recommendations. *Minds and Machines*, *28*(4), 689–707. https://doi.org/10.1007/s11023-018-9482-5

Google AI. (n.d.). *Learn with Google AI*. Google. https://ai.google/education/

Haenlein, M., Kaplan, A., Tan, C.-W., & Zhang, P. (2022). Artificial intelligence (AI) in business and management: State of the art and research agenda. *Journal of Business Research*, *145*, 926–940. https://doi.org/10.1016/j.jbusres.2022.03.027

Topol, E. (2019). *Deep medicine: How artificial intelligence can make healthcare human again*. Basic Books.

Wilson, H. J., Daugherty, P. R., & Davenport, T. H. (2019). The future of work: How artificial intelligence will transform the employee experience. *MIT Sloan Management Review*. https://sloanreview.mit.edu/article/the-future-of-work-how-ai-will-transform-the-employee-experience/

World Economic Forum. (2020). *Jobs of tomorrow: Mapping opportunity in the new economy*. https://www.weforum.org/reports/jobs-of-tomorrow

Chapter Four: Algorithms, Clicks, & Likes

Eubanks, V. (2018). *Automating inequality: How high-tech tools profile, police, and punish the poor*. St. Martin's Press.

Harari, Y. N. (2018). *21 lessons for the 21st century*. Spiegel & Grau.

Lanier, J. (2018). *Ten arguments for deleting your social media accounts right now*. Henry Holt and Company.

O'Neil, C. (2016). *Weapons of math destruction: How big data increases inequality and threatens democracy*. Crown Publishing Group.

Zuboff, S. (2019). *The age of surveillance capitalism: The fight for a human future at the new frontier of power*. PublicAffairs.

Tufekci, Z. (2015). Algorithmic harms beyond Facebook and Google: Emergent challenges of computational agency. *Colorado Technology Law Journal*, *13*(203), 203–218.

Fuchs, C. (2017). *Social media: A critical introduction* (2nd ed.). Sage Publications.

Noble, S. U. (2018). *Algorithms of oppression: How search engines reinforce racism*. NYU Press.

Pariser, E. (2011). *The filter bubble: What the Internet is hiding from you*. Penguin Press.

Anderson, J., & Rainie, L. (2020). *The future of digital life and well-being*. Pew Research Center. https://www.pewresearch.org/internet/2020/10/28/the-future-of-digital-life-and-well-being/

Chapter Five: How AI is Reshaping Our Lives

Brynjolfsson, E., & McAfee, A. (2017). *Machine, platform, crowd: Harnessing our digital future*. W. W. Norton & Company.

Crawford, K. (2021). *Atlas of AI: Power, politics, and the planetary costs of artificial intelligence*. Yale University Press.

Dwivedi, Y. K., Hughes, L., Ismagilova, E., Aarts, G., Coombs, C., Crick, T., ... & Williams, M. D. (2021). Artificial intelligence (AI): Multidisciplinary perspectives on emerging challenges, opportunities, and agenda for research, practice, and policy. *International Journal of Information Management*, 57, 101994. https://doi.org/10.1016/j.ijinfomgt.2019.08.002

Gillespie, T. (2018). *Custodians of the Internet: Platforms, content moderation, and the hidden decisions that shape social media*. Yale University Press.

Heaven, W. D. (2020, October 21). Why deep-learning AIs are so easy to fool. *MIT Technology Review*. https://www.technologyreview.com/2020/10/21/1010945/ai-adversarial-attacks-deep-learning/

Lee, K. F. (2018). *AI superpowers: China, Silicon Valley, and the new world order*. Houghton Mifflin Harcourt.

Marr, B. (2023). *Artificial intelligence in practice: How 50 successful companies used AI and machine learning to solve problems*. Wiley.

O'Neil, C. (2016). *Weapons of math destruction: How big data increases inequality and threatens democracy*. Crown Publishing.

Smith, A. (2024). The AI-powered workplace: Automation, augmentation, and ethics in the new economy. *Harvard Business Review*, 102(4), 48–57.

Sullivan, M. (2023). The ethical implications of AI in healthcare: Bias, privacy, and collaboration. *Journal of Medical Ethics and Technology*, 45(2), 101–110. https://doi.org/10.1136/medethics-2023-1100

Wachter-Boettcher, S. (2017). *Technically wrong: Sexist apps, biased algorithms, and other threats of toxic tech*. W. W. Norton & Company.

West, S. M., Whittaker, M., & Crawford, K. (2019). Discriminating systems: Gender, race, and power in AI. *AI Now Institute*. https://ainowinstitute.org/discriminatingsystems.html

Chapter Six: The Human-AI Power Shift

Creemers, R. (2018). **China's Social Credit System: An Evolving Practice of Control.** *SSRN Electronic Journal.* https://doi.org/10.2139/ssrn.3175792

Deloitte. (2023). **AI Adoption in Financial Services: 2023 Global Report.** Deloitte Insights. https://www2.deloitte.com/global/en/pages/financial-services/articles/ai-in-financial-services.html

Goldman Sachs. (2023). **The Potentially Large Effects of Artificial Intelligence on Economic Growth.** *Goldman Sachs Research.* https://www.goldmansachs.com/intelligence/pages/gs-research/the-potentially-large-effects-of-artificial-intelligence-on-economic-growth/report.pdf

HubSpot. (2024). **The State of AI Marketing: 2024 Report.** HubSpot Research. https://blog.hubspot.com/marketing/state-of-ai-marketing

Isaak, J., & Hanna, M. J. (2018). User Data Privacy: Facebook, Cambridge Analytica, and Privacy Protection. *Computer, 51*(8), 56–59. https://doi.org/10.1109/MC.2018.3191268

Logg, J. M., Minson, J. A., & Moore, D. A. (2019). Algorithm Appreciation: People Prefer Algorithmic to Human Judgment. *Management Science*, *65*(3), 1302–1320. https://doi.org/10.1287/mnsc.2018.3032

McKinsey & Company. (2023). **The Economic Potential of Generative AI: The Next Productivity Frontier.** https://www.mckinsey.com/business-functions/mckinsey-digital/our-insights/the-economic-potential-of-generative-ai

PwC. (2023). **Sizing the Prize: What's the Real Value of AI for Your Business and How Can You Capitalize?** https://www.pwc.com/gx/en/issues/analytics/assets/pwc-ai-analysis-sizing-the-prize-report.pdf

Richardson, R., Schultz, J. M., & Crawford, K. (2019). Dirty Data, Bad Predictions: How Civil Rights Violations Impact Police Data, Predictive Policing Systems, and Justice. *New York University Law Review Online*, *94*, 15–55. https://www.nyulawreview.org/online-features/dirty-data-bad-predictions/

Ross, C., & Swetlitz, I. (2017, September 5). IBM Pitched Its Watson Supercomputer as a Revolution in Cancer Care. It's Nowhere Close. *STAT News.* https://www.statnews.com/2017/09/05/watson-ibm-cancer/

WIPO (World Intellectual Property Organization). (2024). **WIPO Technology Trends 2024: Artificial Intelligence.** https://www.wipo.int/publications/en/details.jsp?id=4560

Zuboff, S. (2019). *The Age of Surveillance Capitalism: The Fight for a Human Future at the New Frontier of Power*. PublicAffairs.

Chapter Seven: AI Knowledge Gaps

Anderson, M., & Auxier, B. (2023, August 28). *How Americans view artificial intelligence*. Pew Research Center. https://www.pewresearch.org/internet/2023/08/28/how-americans-view-artificial-intelligence/

Auxier, B., & Rainie, L. (2023, December 6). *Americans' knowledge of AI: Key findings*. Pew Research Center. https://www.pewresearch.org/internet/2023/12/06/americans-knowledge-of-ai/

Benton Institute for Broadband & Society. (2023). *The state of digital equity: Broadband access and adoption in rural America*. https://www.benton.org/publications/state-digital-equity

BroadbandNow. (2024). *The state of broadband in America: 2024 report*. https://broadbandnow.com/report/us-broadband-2024/

Stanford Institute for Human-Centered Artificial Intelligence. (2024). *Artificial intelligence index report 2024*. Stanford University. https://aiindex.stanford.edu/report/

Nolan, B. (2025). *AI-driven layoffs are on the rise as the job market shrinks for recent grads*. Fortune. https://fortune.com/2025/08/08/ai-layoffs-jobs-market-shrinks-entry-level/

Zhang, B., & Dafoe, A. (2023). Artificial intelligence literacy: A conceptual framework and research agenda. *AI & Society*, 39(1), 151–165. https://doi.org/10.1007/s00146-023-01613-3

National Telecommunications and Information Administration. (2023). *Digital nation data explorer*. U.S. Department of Commerce.

https://www.ntia.doc.gov/data/digital-nation-data-explorer

Chapter Eight: Automation vs. Augmentation

Bessen, J. E. (2015). *Learning by doing: The real connection between innovation, wages, and wealth*. Yale University Press.

Daugherty, P. R., & Wilson, H. J. (2018). *Human + machine: Reimagining work in the age of AI*. Harvard Business Review Press.

McKinsey Global Institute. (2023). *Jobs lost, jobs gained: Workforce transitions in a time of automation*. McKinsey & Company. https://www.mckinsey.com/featured-insights/future-of-work/jobs-lost-jobs-gained-what-the-future-of-work-will-mean-for-jobs-skills-and-wages

O'Neil, C. (2016). *Weapons of math destruction: How big data increases inequality and threatens democracy*. Crown Publishing Group.

Ransbotham, S., Kiron, D., Gerbert, P., & Reeves, M. (2021). The cultural benefits of artificial intelligence in the enterprise. *Harvard Business Review*. https://hbr.org/2021/04/the-cultural-benefits-of-ai-in-the-enterprise

Wilson, H. J., & Daugherty, P. R. (2018). Collaborative intelligence: Humans and AI are joining forces. *Harvard Business Review*. https://hbr.org/2018/07/collaborative-intelligence-humans-and-ai-are-joining-forces

Skinner, B. F. (1972). *Beyond freedom and dignity*. Knopf. *(Quote referenced: "The real question is not whether machines think but whether humans still do.")*

Chapter Nine: Mastering AI Skill Acquisition

Brynjolfsson, E., & McAfee, A. (2014). *The second machine age: Work, progress, and prosperity in a time of brilliant technologies.* W. W. Norton & Company.

Daugherty, P. R., & Wilson, H. J. (2018). *Human + Machine: Reimagining work in the age of AI.* Harvard Business Review Press.

Future of Jobs Report. (2023). *The future of jobs report 2023.* World Economic Forum. https://www.weforum.org/reports/the-future-of-jobs-report-2023

Luckin, R. (2018). *Machine learning and human intelligence: The future of education for the 21st century.* UCL IOE Press.

Marcus, G., & Davis, E. (2019). *Rebooting AI: Building artificial intelligence we can trust.* Pantheon Books.

Microsoft & LinkedIn. (2024). *2024 Work Trend Index: AI at Work is Here. Now Comes the Hard Part.* https://www.microsoft.com/en-us/worklab/work-trend-index/ai-at-work-2024

National Artificial Intelligence Initiative Office. (2023). *National AI R&D strategic plan: 2023 update.* https://www.ai.gov/strategic-plan/

OECD. (2021). *AI and the future of skills, volume 1: Capabilities and assessments.* Organisation for Economic Co-operation and Development. https://doi.org/10.1787/5eeeef7f-en

Russell, S., & Norvig, P. (2021). *Artificial intelligence: A modern approach* (4th ed.). Pearson.

Weller, A. (2019). Transparency: *Understanding and interpreting machine learning models.* In *Proceedings of the 2019 ICML*

Workshop on Human Interpretability in Machine Learning (WHI). https://arxiv.org/abs/1902.02814

Chapter Ten: AI Misinformation

Arntz, M., Gregory, T., & Zierahn, U. (2016). **The Risk of Automation for Jobs in OECD Countries: A Comparative Analysis**. *OECD Social, Employment and Migration Working Papers*, (189). https://doi.org/10.1787/5jlz9h56dvq7-en

Brynjolfsson, E., & McAfee, A. (2014). *The Second Machine Age: Work, Progress, and Prosperity in a Time of Brilliant Technologies*. W. W. Norton & Company.

Chui, M., Manyika, J., & Miremadi, M. (2016). **Where machines could replace humans—and where they can't (yet)**. *McKinsey Quarterly*. https://www.mckinsey.com/business-functions/mckinsey-digital/our-insights/where-machines-could-replace-humans-and-where-they-cant-yet

Davenport, T. H., & Kirby, J. (2016). **Only Humans Need Apply: Winners and Losers in the Age of Smart Machines**. Harper Business.

Frey, C. B., & Osborne, M. A. (2017). **The future of employment: How susceptible are jobs to computerization?** *Technological Forecasting and Social Change, 114*, 254–280. https://doi.org/10.1016/j.techfore.2016.08.019

Wilson, H. J., & Daugherty, P. R. (2018). *Human + Machine: Reimagining Work in the Age of AI*. Harvard Business Review Press.

West, D. M. (2018). **The future of work: Robots, AI, and automation**. Brookings Institution Press.

Bughin, J., Hazan, E., Ramaswamy, S., Chui, M., Allas, T., Dahlström, P., ... & Trench, M. (2018). **Skill shift: Automation and the future of the workforce**. *McKinsey Global Institute.* https://www.mckinsey.com/featured-insights/future-of-work/skill-shift-automation-and-the-future-of-the-workforce

Chapter Eleven: Survival of the Smartest, or the Strongest

World Economic Forum. (2023).

World Economic Forum. (2023). *The Future of Jobs Report 2023.* World Economic Forum. https://www.weforum.org/reports/the-future-of-jobs-report-2023/

McKinsey & Company. (2021).

McKinsey & Company. (2021). *The future of work after COVID-19.* McKinsey Global Institute. https://www.mckinsey.com/featured-insights/future-of-work/the-future-of-work-after-covid-19

McKinsey Global Institute. (2022).

McKinsey Global Institute. (2022). *Defining the skills citizens will need in the future world of work.* McKinsey & Company. https://www.mckinsey.com/capabilities/people-and-organizational-performance/our-insights/defining-the-skills-citizens-will-need-in-the-future-world-of-work

OECD. (2021).

Organisation for Economic Co-operation and Development. (2021). *The OECD Programme for the International Assessment of Adult Competencies (PIAAC): Skills matter.* OECD Publishing. https://doi.org/10.1787/9789264258051-en

Wilson, H. J., & Daugherty, P. R. (2018).

Wilson, H. J., & Daugherty, P. R. (2018). *Collaborative intelligence: Humans and AI are joining forces*. Harvard Business Review. https://hbr.org/2018/07/collaborative-intelligence-humans-and-ai-are-joining-forces

Brynjolfsson, E., & McAfee, A. (2014).

Brynjolfsson, E., & McAfee, A. (2014). *The second machine age: Work, progress, and prosperity in a time of brilliant technologies*. W.W. Norton & Company.

Goleman, D. (1995).

Goleman, D. (1995). *Emotional intelligence: Why it can matter more than IQ*. Bantam Books.

Harari, Y. N. (2018).

Harari, Y. N. (2018). *21 lessons for the 21st century*. Spiegel & Grau.

First Edition Publishing and Copyrights ©2025
by P3 Quality®
2133 Lawrenceville-Suwanee, Ste 12-325, Lawrenceville, Georgia 30024

[U.S. Copyright Issue date, 09.13.2022]
Official USPTO Trademark Notice of Publication Under 12(a)
[U.S. Trademark Issue date, 02.25.2025]

Library of Congress Cataloging Review and Approval **[Pending]**

E-Book ISBN: (979-8-9930558-2-4)
ISBN Paperback: (979-8-9930558-0-0)
ISBN Hardcover: (979-8-9930558-1-7)

Typeset In:
Title: Artificial Intelligence, Rise, Survive & Thrive in an AI-Powered World

ABOUT THE AUTHOR

Corliss Willett Collins, also called (Ms. Co Co), is a visionary thought leader at the intersection of Artificial Intelligence, Healthcare Revenue Cycle Management (RCM), and Digital Transformation. With over fifteen years of experience working with AI-Powered Technologies, in organizations as they navigate through the complexities of AI in RCM integration. Ms. Co Co is becoming a trusted voice in AI literacy, quality, compliance, and ethical innovation.

As a Certified AI Medical Coder, Certified AI Professional, Nationally Certified Business Owner, Founder, and CEO of a Patent-Pending AI Technology. Ms. Co Co is dedicated to helping individuals, professionals, and businesses not only navigate but also thrive in an AI-powered world. Her Vision is to bridge the gap between technology and humanity, recommending practical strategies for adopting AI while preserving integrity, transparency, and human wisdom.

In addition to developing an AI-powered technology within the healthcare revenue cycle management (RCM) industry, Ms. Co Co serves as a Subject Matter Expert on the American Institute of Healthcare Compliance (AIHC) Education Committee.

Join the movement to lead with wisdom in this AI-powered world.

www.ingramcontent.com/pod-product-compliance
Lightning Source LLC
LaVergne TN
LVHW022112200926
848481LV00003B/1155
* 9 7 9 8 9 9 3 0 5 5 8 0 0 *